Second

"*Second Chance, Second Act* brings us practical wisdom and enduring hope to move us in a positive direction. In his brilliant and delightful writing style, Dr. Robert Jeffress points us to the restoration and redemption God can bring into our life no matter what the circumstances."

—KAROL LADD, author, *The Power of a Positive Woman*

"Everyone needs a new beginning at one time or another. Dr. Robert Jeffress, a gifted writer and positive communicator, renews hope and provides vital insights on how you can make a comeback from failures and setbacks in life. This book will help you to make the best of a mess you never intended. You really can begin again!"

—DR. DAVID H. MCKINLEY, teaching pastor, Prestonwood
   Baptist Church, Plano, Texas

"Job doesn't have to be the only one whose life was better at the end than the beginning. This practical, biblical guide shows how to recover from mistakes and make your second act worthy of a standing ovation!"

—JUNE HUNT, founder and CEO, Hope for the Heart

Praise for
The Divine Defense

"I highly recommend this latest from one of Christianity's leading pastor-teachers...a clear and practical battle strategy for the ideals we hold sacred."

—DR. ED YOUNG, pastor, Second Baptist Church in Houston,
   Texas, and author of *Romancing the Home* and *The Ten
   Commandments of Marriage*

"If you can only read one book this year, this is it, and for all your remaining years of spiritual service, you will be glad you did."

—CHAPLAIN (COL.) GIL A. STRICKLIN, USA, retired; founder and president, Marketplace Chaplains USA and International

"A book about truths that should be both in our heads and hearts to prepare us for spiritual battle. Intensively biblical. Useful in the day by day. One book I'm sure to reread on numerous occasions."

—DR. MARK L. BAILEY, president, Dallas Theological Seminary

"A balanced look at spiritual warfare, giving a concrete plan for success in the spirit realm."

—RANDY SINGER, author of *The Cross Examination of Jesus Christ* and its companion novel, *The Cross Examination of Oliver Finney*

"Struggling with life's challenges? *The Divine Defense* identifies the enemy, exposes his strategies, reinforces our defenses, and motivates us to victory. Don't miss this book with what you need to know to win!"

—DR. ED HINDSON, assistant chancellor, Liberty University

"A great resource for Christians living in a fast-paced world. You will be reminded as to the why of the distress in and around you as well as the how to mute the agitation. The truth is our enemy doesn't have a prayer—and this book will help you practice that truth."

—NEIL ATKINSON, author of *The Shrewd Christian*

"A biblical and balanced approach to dealing with Satan and defeating spiritual enemies…[and] a call to arms that we may experience true victory in Jesus."

—DR. JACK GRAHAM, pastor, Prestonwood Baptist Church, and author with Chuck Norris of *A Man of God*

SECOND CHANCE, SECOND ACT

TURNING YOUR MESSES INTO SUCCESSES

ROBERT JEFFRESS

WATERBROOK
PRESS

SECOND CHANCE, SECOND ACT
PUBLISHED BY WATERBROOK PRESS
12265 Oracle Boulevard, Suite 200
Colorado Springs, Colorado 80921
A division of Random House Inc.

All Scripture quotations, unless otherwise indicated, are taken from the New American Standard Bible®. © Copyright The Lockman Foundation 1960, 1962, 1963, 1968, 1971, 1972, 1973, 1975, 1977, 1995. Used by permission. (www.Lockman.org). Scripture quotations marked (KJV) are taken from the King James Version. Scripture taken from The Message by Eugene H. Peterson. Copyright © 1993, 1994, 1995, 1996, 2000, 2001, 2002. Used by permission of NavPress Publishing Group. All rights reserved. Scripture quotations marked (NIV) are taken from the Holy Bible, New International Version®. NIV®. Copyright © 1973, 1978, 1984 by the International Bible Society. Used by permission of Zondervan Publishing House. All rights reserved. Scripture quotations marked (NLT) are taken from the Holy Bible, New Living Translation, copyright © 1996, 2004. Used by permission of Tyndale House Publishers Inc., Carol Stream, Illinois 60188. All rights reserved.

Quotations from "Reconstructing Woody" reprinted by permission of International Creative Management Inc. Copyright © 2005 by Peter Biskind.

Details in some anecdotes and stories have been changed to protect the identities of the persons involved.

ISBN 978-1-4000-7091-6

Published in association with Yates & Yates, LLP, Attorneys and Counselors, Orange, California.

Library of Congress Cataloging-in-Publication Data
Jeffress, Robert, 1955-
    Second chance, second act : turning your messes into successes / Robert Jeffress.
        p. cm.
    Includes bibliographical references.
    ISBN 978-1-4000-7091-6
    1. Failure (Psychology)—Religious aspects—Christianity. I. Title.
    BT730.5.J44 2007
    248.8'6—dc22
                                    2006102198

Printed in the United States of America
2007—First Edition

10 9 8 7 6 5 4 3 2 1

To Hollis and Donna Sullivan

Thank you for your faithful stewardship of the resources
God has entrusted to you
as you help us spread the message of Christ around the world.
You are an incomparable encouragement to your pastor.

Contents

ACT 1

Messed Up, Not Washed Up

When You Think It's Curtains!

Waiting anxiously for my flight to be called so I could return home, I decided to make one final stop in the rest room. I was washing my hands when I glanced over and saw a woman entering the bathroom. She froze in her tracks upon seeing me at the sink and began to apologize profusely.

"I'm so sorry," she said.

"That's all right. It happens to me all the time," I replied, trying to alleviate her obvious embarrassment.

I finished drying my hands, brushed my hair, and straightened my tie before leaving. For some reason I glanced back and noticed an unexpected image to the side of the rest-room door I'd just exited: a feminine stick figure accompanied by the word Women.

I was the one who had been in the wrong rest room the entire time!

We all make mistakes almost every hour of every day. I'm sure you have a number of embarrassing moments you could share as well.

However, I imagine the reason you picked up this book is not because of some minor mishap, like entering the wrong rest room. More likely, in your distant or immediate past is one whopper of a mistake that haunts you.

An innocent friendship that turned into a torrid affair.

A poor financial decision that threatens your future security.

An opportunity you squandered because of sheer laziness.

A choice to invest more time in your career than in your family.

A decision to end a relationship you should have stayed in.

A decision to stay in a relationship you should have ended.

Your mistake, with its accompanying and unending regrets, raises all kinds of questions in your mind.

"Can my mistake ever be forgiven?"

"Even if I'm forgiven of my mistake, will I still spend the rest of my life paying for it?"

"If God planned every detail of my life before I was born, did His plan include the mistake I made?"

"Can I totally recover from my mistake?"

As the old joke begins, I have good news and bad news. The bad news is that you can't rewrite history. You can't really start over because life has no Rewind button. The good news is that your mistake can actually be a steppingstone to greater success in life.

That's what this book is all about.

American novelist F. Scott Fitzgerald once wrote, "There are no second acts in American lives."

He was wrong. You can recover from your mistakes and enjoy a great second act in your life. Your biggest mess can be transformed into your greatest success by applying the principles from God's Word we are going to discover in this book.

As a prelude to our discussion, there are three important truths we need to understand.

EVERYBODY MAKES MISTAKES

When my daughter Julia was three, she was a regular fan of the television program *Sesame Street* (as were her parents, who appreciated the much-needed electronic childcare). During that period, whenever I confronted Julia about her misbehavior, she would rationalize her disobedience by paraphrasing one of Big Bird's signature lines: "Well, Dad, 'everybody makes mistakes.'"

Big Bird was right. We all make mistakes. You've probably heard a litany of famous mistakes in history.

The executive who introduced New Coke to the world in the 1980s.

The creative geniuses at Decca Records who passed up signing the Beatles to a contract.

The numerous movie studios that rejected a script entitled *Star Wars*.

The automobile company that produced the Edsel.

Author Stephen Pile listed a number of those failures in a book called *The Incomplete Book of Failures*. But when the book was released, two pages were missing![1]

We all make mistakes, including people who write books about mistakes. Our mistakes tend to come in three sizes: slip-ups, mess-ups, and blowups.

Slip-Ups

A few years ago, my wife and I sped to the airport after our Sunday morning worship services to catch a flight for a seminar we were scheduled to attend. Knowing we didn't have much time, I pulled up to the front of the terminal, quickly unloaded the luggage from the trunk, and raced to the ticket counter. Fortunately, we made it just in time. Once on board we settled into our seats, caught our breath, and talked about the coming week.

After arriving at our hotel and enjoying a late dinner, I called my associate pastor to see how the evening service had gone. "Fine," he said. Then he added, almost as an afterthought, "By the way, Pastor, did you happen to forget something before you left?"

"No, I can't think of anything," I replied, wondering where this was going.

He began to laugh. "This afternoon we received a call from the airport saying an unattended blue Buick LeSabre had been left in front of the airport with its engine running, doors open, and trunk lid up. The police were concerned and checked the car registration and said it was yours." Ooops!

Slip-ups are those small mistakes that carry few consequences (other than being rehashed by church staff and lay people for years

6

to come, as mine is). Failing to mail a bill on time, leaving the sprinkler system on overnight, or forgetting to pick up the dry cleaning before the weekend causes temporary inconvenience and embarrassment, but no one loses sleep over it.

Mess-Ups

These are mistakes that result in more painful consequences. This week I met with a couple who had made a terrible financial blunder. Driving around a new neighborhood one Sunday afternoon, they spotted a beautiful house that instantly became their dream home. Assured by friends and an eager real-estate agent that this house would not remain on the market long and that their current residence would sell in an instant, they purchased the new house before they sold their current residence.

Now, six months later, they are still the not-so-proud owners of two homes and are at the end of their financial rope. Wondering when their financial bleeding from making two house payments will end, they ask, "Why did God allow us to make such a poor decision? Why won't He answer our prayers to sell our home?"

Obviously, this couple exercised poor judgment, violating important biblical admonitions against presuming upon the future and incurring debt without a sure way to repay it. Now they are experiencing the fallout of their choices.

Although their mistake is painful, it is also temporary. Eventually they will sell their home, even if it is not at the price they desired. One day they will climb out of their financial hole, will replenish their depleted cash reserves, and will have learned an important lesson.

Blowups

These are monumental mistakes that seem to carry unending negative consequences. While on a brief business trip, Jerry met Sara at an industry trade show. You can probably write the rest of the story. Their one night of passion led to an affair that lasted for three years.

Dana, Jerry's wife, discovered the affair through a hotel receipt in Jerry's pocket and issued an ultimatum. "End this relationship immediately, or I'm leaving," she threatened.

Jerry confessed his adultery, asked for Dana's forgiveness, and broke off the relationship with Sara.

But Jerry's repentance hasn't produced the results he desired. Dana regularly reminds Jerry of his unfaithfulness. Jerry and Dana's sex life is sporadic and unsatisfactory. He feels alienated from God and wonders if every mishap he experiences is evidence of God's displeasure toward him.

He would give anything if he could erase the decision to invite Sara to his room that night. But he can't, and he feels as if he will spend the rest of his life paying for that momentous mistake.

Have you experienced your own serious blowup?

Confession time is in order here.

I've experienced my share in my past…and I imagine you have too. Our biggest mistakes and missteps may involve a lapse in moral judgment that led to an affair, an abortion, or a divorce. But there are other kinds of failures beyond mistakes of morality. Perhaps your blowup involved a poor choice for which you're still paying: You accepted a job offer that seemed very appealing at the time, but it resulted in a move that has been disastrous for your children. Or you decided to ignore the warning signs of a potential health problem, but after giving in to your mate's relentless urging to see a doctor, you discover that your problem is real and perhaps irreversible. Or maybe you chose to marry an individual who appeared to be exactly the kind of mate for which you had been searching. But after the "I do's," you discovered some serious character flaws in your mate that have made life miserable for you.

Sometimes the most painful mistakes we make aren't what we do but what we fail to do.

Missed opportunities. The unending costs of rearing children and unexpected emergencies cause you to postpone putting money into your 401(k) retirement plan until one day you awaken to the fact that you are only a few years from retirement. Or you finally have the time and money to take that vacation with your children that you've talked about for years, but now they have neither the time nor the desire to go with you. Maybe the demands of your job keep you from spending quality time with your mate. *One day when life settles down, we will have all the time in the world to spend together,* you think. But that "one day" is supplanted by a terrible day when your mate is unexpectedly taken from you.

Several years ago I was on a program with motivational speaker Les Brown, who made an observation that I jotted down on an index card as quickly as I could: "The richest ground on planet earth is not found in the diamond fields of South Africa or the oil fields of West Texas. The richest ground on earth is the cemetery, for in it we find bodies containing speeches that were never given, books that were never written, songs that were never sung, and dreams that were never fulfilled."[2]

Forfeited opportunities. These are particularly painful because they seem to be the most irreversible mistakes. In the movie *The Mirror Has Two Faces,* the mother character—played by Lauren Bacall—laments, "It's an awful thing to look back on life and realize that you have settled. The thing is that you feel like you have more time, and then you one day wake up and realize that most of your life is behind you."

We can't turn the clock backward and regain opportunities we've squandered, remake choices we regret, or redo parts of our lives we are embarrassed about.

However, before you reach for the revolver and decide to end it all, there is some good news you need to consider.

MISTAKES ARE FORGIVABLE

Why do we consistently experience slip-ups, mess-ups, and blow-ups? What is it inside of us that pulls us toward the wrong choices in life?

In a word: sin.

As the New Testament writer Paul said, "All have sinned and fall short of the glory of God" (Romans 3:23).

The word *sin* means "to miss the mark." In other words, all of us fail to hit the bull's-eye of perfection 100 percent of the time— even most of the time. We all fall short of the ideal for our marriages, our personal lives, our work, our financial decisions, and our relationship to God.

Where did our natural inclination to make mistakes originate? The apostle Paul explains:

Therefore, just as through one man [Adam] sin entered into the world, and death through sin, and so death spread to all men, because all sinned. (Romans 5:12)

I don't pretend to understand the mechanics of how it happened, but what happened is clear: you and I have inherited a predisposition to mess up from our great-great-great-great-great-grandparents, Adam and Eve. Their initial mistake in the Garden of Eden ensured that every one of their offspring would also be inclined to make mistakes.

Although we are not the ones who were responsible for the initial choice to sin, we must live with the consequences of that choice. We inhabit bodies that have been contaminated with an inclination toward slip-ups, mess-ups, and blowups or, as the Bible calls them, "sin."

Now I can hear some of you saying, "That's not fair. Why should I have to suffer the consequences for someone else's mistake?"

Perhaps this illustration will help. A few years ago we discovered that our home, like many other homes in Texas, had been contaminated with mold. The experts who examined the house told us that if we didn't go through an expensive process of removing the mold, we could become ill and even die. Although we weren't responsible for the formation of the mold, we did have to suffer the consequences of it.

Fortunately, we had an insurance company that would cover the tremendous cost of moving us to another residence for nearly a year while builders gutted and rebuilt much of our home. So when we were informed of the condition of our home, we had a choice to make. We could stay in our house and take our chances, arguing that it wasn't fair for us to suffer the inconvenience of moving because of a problem we weren't responsible for. Or we could accept the insurance company's offer to renovate our home free of charge.

Although it was unfair that we were forced to suffer the fallout from the mold, it was perhaps even more unfair that the insurance company had to pay a huge sum of money for a problem it didn't cause.

You and I inhabit bodies that have been contaminated with sin and predispose us to continually make wrong choices for which we must experience both temporary and eternal consequences. While it may seem unjust that we are held responsible for Adam and Eve's mistake, God does offer us a way out. He paid the cost of forgiving our sins and renovating our lives by sending Christ to die for us. The only thing more unfair than our being held responsible for Adam's mistake is our being forgiven because of Jesus's perfection.

> For the sin of this one man, Adam, brought death to many.
> But even greater is God's wonderful grace and his gift of
> forgiveness to many through this other man, Jesus Christ.
> And the result of God's gracious gift is very different from
> the result of that one man's sin. For Adam's sin led to con-
> demnation, but God's free gift leads to our being made
> right with God, even though we are guilty of many sins.
> (Romans 5:15–16, NLT)

Unlike the insurance company, which was contractually obligated to pay for the renovation of my home, God had no obligation to pay for our mistakes and the renovation of our lives. There's only one reason God offers to forgive you.

Grace.

"An undeserved burst of God's generosity," as I define it.

In spite of your slip-ups, mess-ups, and blowups, God not only loves you, but He likes you. A lot.

Recently I was told of a teenager who was in an institution for a severe eating disorder. She'd become extremely withdrawn, and her family feared she might never recover. A friend wondered if I might write her a note of encouragement. These words from Max Lucado immediately came to mind:

> There are many reasons God saves you: to bring glory to himself, to appease his justice, to demonstrate his sovereignty. But one of the sweetest reasons God saved you is because he is fond of you. He likes having you around. He thinks you are the best thing to come down the pike in quite awhile....
>
> If God had a refrigerator, your picture would be on it. If he had a wallet, your photo would be in it. He sends you flowers every spring and a sunrise every morning. Whenever you want to talk, he'll listen. He can live anywhere in the universe, and he chose your heart.... Face it, friend. He's crazy about you.[3]

You will never be able to move beyond your mistakes until you realize that God is willing to move beyond your mistakes. " 'Come now, and let us reason together,' says the LORD, 'though your sins are as scarlet, they will be as white as snow' " (Isaiah 1:18).

In the next chapter we will discover how to experience God's forgiveness for our mistakes.

MISTAKES DON'T HAVE TO UNDO YOU

Mistakes are inevitable because we've inherited a bent toward doing stupid things, and we can't undo our mistakes. But our mistakes are forgivable. God offers to let us off the eternal hook for our failures by His willingness to allow His Son, Jesus, to suffer the punishment we deserve.

If God's forgiveness of our mistakes resulted only in our not going to hell for all eternity, that would certainly be more grace than we deserve. Think about it. Even if an affair cost you your family, a financial mistake wiped out your savings, a forfeited opportunity resulted in years of regret, or a crime resulted in your life imprisonment, but you still escaped an eternity of suffering the torment of hell, would you argue that God had not done enough for you?

Just as God is under no obligation to offer you grace to free you from the eternal consequences of your mistakes, He is under no obligation to provide you with anything beyond that invaluable Get Out of Hell Free card. But that doesn't stop Him! God's undeserved generosity—grace—affects our lives on this side of the grave as well.

God's grace can actually transform your worst mistakes into a prelude for a great second act in your life. God can turn the bitter into sweet. Do you have a hard time believing that? Consider...

Abraham, who at one time was a worshiper of idols. Even after his spiritual conversion, he had sex with his wife's servant and

14

allowed his spouse to be taken captive to save his own skin. Nevertheless, Abraham was known as God's friend.

Noah, who in a drunken romp disgraced himself in front of his sons. Yet Noah "found grace in the eyes of the LORD" (Genesis 6:8, KJV).

Rahab, who was a prostitute. Nevertheless, she played a pivotal role in the conquest of Jericho and is named as one of Jesus's ancestors.

Peter, who in spite of all his promises to the contrary, denied that he had even heard of Jesus the night before His crucifixion. Yet the Lord chose him to be the leader of the apostles.

Paul, who regularly blasphemed the name of Christ and imprisoned and murdered the followers of Christ. Yet he was transformed into the greatest missionary the world has ever known.

God offers to do the same for you and your mistakes, if you will let Him.

YOUR PULSE IS YOUR GREATEST PLUS

Take your right hand, place it over your heart, and repeat "I pledge allegiance…"

No, just kidding. But keep your hand there for a moment.

Feel the beat?

It means you're alive. In spite of your mistakes, God didn't kill you, though He had every right to do so. Instead, He has given you the marvelous gift of time to recover from your failures and enjoy a great second act in your life.

But why would He do that?

15

MEET THE DIVINE DIRECTOR

C arlo Walth made a life-changing mistake from which there appeared to be no recovery. Carlo was a veteran youth minister serving a growing church in Northern California. Over a period of time, he had developed what he called a "special friendship" with one of the girls in the youth ministry. He excused his emotional attachment to the girl by saying that she was a special sister whom he could influence and disciple. Carlo looked forward to seeing her regularly and speaking to her on the phone.

Carlo's pastor became concerned after hearing a complaint from another family in the church who sensed something wasn't right. Convinced he was doing nothing wrong, Carlo brushed off the pastor's concern and similarly dismissed his wife's growing anxiety over the relationship.

One day everything unraveled. Several notes Carlo had written the girl, coaching her on how to respond when questioned about their relationship, were discovered. Even though Carlo and the girl had not been physically involved, their emotional relationship destroyed his credibility with the church and severely damaged his relationship with his wife.

Carlo was immediately fired and asked to discontinue any contact with the church.

"And so began two of the most difficult years of my life," Carlo later wrote.

> At first I tried to hide. I wouldn't go to a restaurant or a store in our town. I changed vehicles, because many knew me and recognized the truck I'd been driving around town for five years. For a couple of months I couldn't even pull myself together enough to try attending church anywhere. Then one day driving with my family, my wife was expressing her grief and pain, and I nearly lost it. I parked our vehicle and started walking down a street in an unfamiliar town. I didn't think I'd be coming back. It was the only time in my life I was truly tempted to end my life—or just disappear.[1]

Perhaps in your past is a mistake that may have caused you to want to end your life or at least caused you to wish you could start over. Your mistake may have been one of poor judgment, squandered opportunity, or overt disobedience to God. Perhaps, like

Carlo's, your mistake has already been publicly revealed, exposing you to tremendous embarrassment. Or your mistake may still be hidden from public view...at least for now.

Regardless of the nature of your mistake, you wonder if it has become the defining event of your life. Will you spend the rest of your years suffering the fallout from your poor choice, or is it possible that you can move beyond your failure?

The answer to that question depends on two—and only two— living beings: you and God.

We can experience a second act only if the Divine Director is willing to give us another chance after our first-act mistake. After all, as the creator, writer, and producer of the seventy- to eighty-year drama we call life, He certainly has the right to end the show anytime He chooses.

The apostle Paul asked the question, "If God be for us, who can be against us?" (Romans 8:31, KJV). The implication is obvious. Having God as your advocate is like having the biggest kid on the playground as your best friend. As long as He is on your side, no one and nothing can harm you.

But the opposite is also true. If God is against you, nothing else really matters. If He refuses to let you off the hook for your mistake, then there is no hope for a new beginning in life.

So the foundational question each of us must answer before going any further is simple: is God willing to forgive my failure?

In order to move from the theoretical to the practical, I want you to picture the single biggest mistake you've ever made. I'm talking about the most explosive blowups in your life. If you were

19

going to select one incident from your past that you would hate to have projected on a big screen for your mate, children, and closest friends to view, this would be the one.

Isn't it amazing how quickly most of us can identify that mistake? Now that you have your mistake clearly in mind, I'll pose the question again. Is God willing to forgive you for *that* mistake?

Let's allow God to answer that question for Himself. Look at a few of the statements God has made in His Word about His willingness to forgive:

> "In an outburst of anger
> I hid My face from you for a moment;
> But with everlasting lovingkindness I will have compassion
>   on you,"
> Says the LORD your Redeemer. (Isaiah 54:8)

> I will forgive their iniquity, and their sin I will remember no more. (Jeremiah 31:34)

> Now return to the LORD your God,
> For He is gracious and compassionate,
> Slow to anger, abounding in lovingkindness. (Joel 2:13)

> As far as the east is from the west,
> So far has He removed our transgressions from us.
>   (Psalm 103:12)

WHAT IS FORGIVENESS?

To forgive means "to release, to let go of." If someone hurts you, you have a choice about your response to the offense. You can hold on to it and demand your pound of flesh from the offender. Or you can choose to release your offender from his wrong. Forgiving means surrendering your right to hurt someone for hurting you.

Our willingness and ability to forgive others is directly linked to God's willingness to forgive us. "Be kind to one another, tenderhearted, forgiving each other, just as God in Christ also has forgiven you," the Bible commands (Ephesians 4:32). Think about the last few words of that sentence for a moment: "just as God in Christ also has forgiven you." God offers to release you from the offenses you have committed against Him—every lie you have ever told, every impure thought you have ever entertained, every time you have placed your desires above His desires. Even though you and I deserve hell for what we have done, God offers us heaven instead. He's surrendered His right to get even.

THE BASIS FOR OUR FORGIVENESS

Some people are rather nonchalant about God's offer to forgive. They're grateful God has let them off the hook and has decided not to send them to hell. But what's the big deal? After all, every day you and I overlook the faults of others. We don't regularly slug our boss when he mistreats us, curse our mate when he ignores us, or kill our children when they disobey us. Shouldn't we expect God to do the nice thing and turn the other cheek as well?

But God's not like us. He is perfect, and because He is perfect, He can't tolerate imperfection. That's why "the LORD will by no means leave the guilty unpunished" (Nahum 1:3).

That's not particularly good news for us, because as we saw in the last chapter, we all fall in the "guilty" category:

We've all fallen short of the ideal.

We've all missed the mark.

We've all fouled up.

We all deserve hell.

So here's the $64,000 question: how can a perfect God let imperfect people off the hook if He's obligated to punish mistakes?

Only God could have fashioned a solution for such a dilemma—and here it is:

He made [Jesus] who knew no sin to be sin on our behalf,
so that we might become the righteousness of God in Him.
(2 Corinthians 5:21)

Jesus Christ is the only person who couldn't relate to the subject matter of this book. He never made a mistake. He never experienced a blowup, mess-up, or even a slip-up. He was perfect.

Nevertheless, Jesus chose to take the punishment we deserve from God for our mistakes. He felt the full brunt of God's anger when He hung on the cross in our place. He accepted the full blast of God's wrath on our behalf. God did not—because He could not—simply overlook our sin. Somebody had to pay for our mistakes. And that Someone was Jesus.

So how does Jesus's death cover our failures?

Max Lucado illustrates the answer by describing an experience with his daughter that most parents can relate to.

The bank sent me an overdraft notice on the checking account of one of my daughters. I encourage my college-age girls to monitor their accounts. Even so, they sometimes overspend.

What should I do? Let the bank absorb it? They won't. Send her an angry letter? Admonition might help her later, but it won't satisfy the bank. Phone and tell her to make a deposit? Might as well tell a fish to fly. I know her liquidity. Zero.

Transfer the money from my account to hers? Seemed to be the best option. After all, I had $25.37. I could replenish her account and pay the overdraft fee as well.

Besides, that's my job. Don't get any ideas. If you're overdrawn, don't call me. My daughter can do something you can't do: she can call me Dad. And since she calls me Dad, I did what dads do. I covered my daughter's mistake.

When I told her she was overdrawn, she said she was sorry. Still, she offered no deposit. She was broke. She had one option. "Dad, could you..." I interrupted her sentence. "Honey, I already have." I met her need before she knew she had one.

Long before you knew you needed grace, your Father did the same. He made the deposit, an ample deposit. "Christ died for us while we were still sinners" (Rom. 5:8 NCV). Before you knew you needed a Savior, you had one. And when you ask him for mercy, he answers, "I've already given it, dear child. I've already given it."[2]

All of us are overdrawn in our goodness account. We've all come up short. But we have a Father willing to make up the deficit for us if we're willing to ask. When we say, "God, I'm sorry for my failures. Do you think you could possibly...," He replies, *I've already done it. That's why I sent Christ to die for you.*

I realize we are wading through some deep theological waters here.

However, the fact that Jesus willingly endured the punishment we deserve for our mistakes has two practical ramifications for us.

WE'RE FREE FROM GOD'S CONDEMNATION

We don't have to experience hell for our sins, because Jesus already has experienced hell for us. Our mistakes demand a payment—but only one payment. Nobody needs to pay twice.

For example, imagine that your teenager comes to you with a problem. "I got a speeding ticket last week, and I don't have the money to pay it," he says. "If I don't come up with the cash, I'll lose my license or go to jail."

What do you do?

Out of love for your child, you pay the fine for him, right?

But later in the month, when he receives an unexpected birthday check in the mail from Aunt Ethel, would he under any circumstances use that money to pay the fine a second time?

Of course not!

One payment is enough.

Those who have allowed Christ to pay for their mistakes never need to worry about having to pay again themselves. One payment is enough. Some of Jesus's final words from the cross were "It is finished" (John 19:30), which actually means "paid in full."

We can do nothing to add to the once-for-all-payment Christ made for our sins.

I'm not suggesting that Christ's death automatically removes all the temporary consequences of our mistakes. Terminations, divorces, humiliation, and even imprisonment may be part of the fallout you and I experience whenever we fail to live up to God's standards.

So what difference does God's forgiveness make if it doesn't exempt us from experiencing painful consequences for our mistakes?

Simple.

Thirty years of suffering in this life sure beats thirty billion trillion years—and more—of suffering in the next life!

Whenever I think of someone who endured painful consequences for a major blowup in his life, King David comes to mind. One night of unbridled passion resulted in a lifetime of sorrow that included a dead child, a divided kingdom, a disloyal son, and a disgraced reputation. Nevertheless, the realization that he was forever free of God's condemnation for his sin led David to exclaim,

> How blessed is he whose transgression is *forgiven,*
> Whose sin is *covered!*
> How blessed is the man to whom the LORD does not
> > *impute* iniquity. (Psalm 32:1–2, emphasis added)

26

How could David be so excited about his situation when he would have to spend the rest of his life experiencing the consequences of his mistake?

Three words David uses in these verses explain why he had a reason to be so happy (the meaning of the word translated *blessed*).

Forgiven. The Hebrew word translated *forgiven* means "to separate." When God forgives us, He separates us from our sin. For all our talk about "hating the sin but loving the sinner," we mortals are rarely able to pull that off.

For example, think about someone who has hurt you deeply. I imagine a name has already popped into your mind. Do you ever see this person without immediately thinking about his offense toward you? Do you ever hear his name without reliving a little of the pain he brought into your life? It's nearly impossible for us to separate a person from his sin.

In biblical times, a murderer would be bound to his crime for the rest of his life—literally. For punishment, the victim's corpse would be tied to the killer so that he was forced to carry the decaying body with him until the day he died. The sinner was bound to his sin.

But when God forgives us, He separates us from our crime. One of the greatest illustrations of that truth is seen in the Jewish day of atonement. Before the high priest would enter the holy of holies, he would confess the sins of the people over the head of a goat, called the scapegoat. The goat was then sent into the wilderness, never to be seen again.

That's what God does with our sin when He forgives us. Jesus Christ is the scapegoat who takes our sin out of God's view...forever. "As far as the east is from the west, so far has He removed our transgressions from us," the psalmist declared (Psalm 103:12).

History, on the other hand, is very unforgiving. The captain of the *Titanic* will always be remembered for steering the great ocean liner into an iceberg. Benedict Arnold will always be remembered as a traitor to his country. Richard Nixon will always be remembered as the first president to resign in disgrace. Janet Jackson will always be remembered for her Super Bowl wardrobe malfunction.

Maybe you have a friend—or even a mate—who seems to have majored in history, because he or she is constantly reminding you of your past failures. You wonder if you will ever be seen apart from your mistakes. The good news is that God separated you from your failure the moment you asked for His forgiveness.

Covered. God's forgiveness not only separates us from our sin, it also covers over our sin. Frankly, allowing God to cover our mistakes is much easier and much more effective than trying to cover over them ourselves. When the wife of Chico Marx, of the famed Marx brothers, caught him kissing a chorus girl, he quickly explained, "I wasn't kissing her. I was whispering in her mouth." I doubt Mrs. Marx was satisfied with the explanation.

While it's difficult to hide your mistakes from other people, it's impossible to hide them from God. But that doesn't stop us from trying, does it? The desire to sweep our mistakes under the carpet is part of our basic DNA that wastes a lot of energy, as we will see in chapter 4. But more important, covering over our mistakes never works.

One of my wife's pet peeves is my Saturday-night routine of polishing my shoes in front of the television set. Even though I carefully unfold some newspapers on top of the carpet, some specks of shoe polish invariably end up on the carpet. I immediately retrieve a can of special stain remover, spray it on the soiled carpet, gently rub the solution over the spot, and watch it magically disappear—for about a minute, before it reappears…at which time I disappear into another part of the house until the marital storm blows over.

David spent months trying to cover over his sin with Bathsheba with rationalization ("The king can do whatever he wants. It's good to be the king!") and even murder by ordering the death of Bathsheba's husband. But nothing worked. The black spot of sin kept reappearing in David's conscience, as well as in view of the entire kingdom. Only when David cried out to God, "Purify me…and I shall be clean. Wash me, and I shall be whiter than snow" (Psalm 51:7), did he experience the relief that comes from allowing God to cover a mistake.

Impute. God's forgiveness meant that He would no longer "impute iniquity." The word *impute* is an accounting term that means to charge to someone's account. For example, let's say that because of some financial mistakes, you file for bankruptcy and ruin your credit rating. Every time you apply for a loan, the lender looks at your credit rating, sees the bankruptcy, and gives you that "you've got to be kidding" look.

However, you have a friend who works at the credit-reporting agency and offers to help. With one stroke of the computer, he makes the bankruptcy disappear from your record. Your failure is no longer imputed, or charged, to your account.

But then your friend goes a step further. "With another stroke of a computer key, I'm going to give you Bill Gates's credit rating. Every time people look up your credit score, they'll see the rating for America's richest man!" your friend offers. From that point on, anytime you apply for a loan, the lender's only question is "How much money would you like?"

When God forgives you, He performs a similar transaction on your behalf. He no longer counts your spiritual bankruptcy against you. When you die and stand before God, you never have to worry that He is going to look at your record and say, *I think you've come to the wrong place.*

But beyond that, God has done something even more remarkable. He has taken the perfect record of His Son, Jesus Christ, and credited it to your account. In God's eyes, you are a spiritual billionaire.

No wonder David was so ecstatic over God's forgiveness!

WE CAN EXPERIENCE A RADICAL TRANSFORMATION

Your greatest failure doesn't have to be your grand finale. God's willingness to forgive your mistake results in more than simply wiping the slate clean and allowing you a fresh start. God is able to transform any mess into success.

I can only imagine what you're thinking: *Robert, that sounds like a lot of positive thinking mumbo jumbo. I realize that God can forgive my mistakes—but actually use my mistakes for good? No way!*

Jeremiah the prophet also had difficulty accepting that possibility until God sent him on a field trip to learn an important lesson. Let Jeremiah tell the rest of the story:

> Then I went down to the potter's house, and there he was,
> making something on the wheel. But the vessel that he
> was making of clay was spoiled in the hand of the potter;
> so he remade it into another vessel, as it pleased the potter
> to make. (Jeremiah 18:3–4)

If a potter found a flaw in the clay while forming a pot, he usually threw the clay into the potter's field and started over with a new lump of clay.

Not this potter. He was too thrifty to waste a perfectly good clump of clay. Instead of discarding the clay, he reshaped it—including all of its imperfections—into the kind of vessel he wanted.

In case Jeremiah missed the point, God continued:

> Can I not, O house of Israel, deal with you as this potter
> does?…Behold, like the clay in the potter's hand, so are
> you in My hand, O house of Israel. (Jeremiah 18:6)

In spite of Israel's acts of disobedience, the Lord didn't abandon His people. He used Israel's monumental mistakes (including the crucifixion of God's own Son) to accomplish His ultimate purpose. God reshaped evil into good.

God offers to do the same for you.

No matter the size or scope of your mistake, God can not only forgive it, but He can reshape it for your good and His glory. In fact, the bigger the mistake, the bigger the opportunity God has to demonstrate His willingness to forgive and His power to transform.

As Gordon MacDonald writes, God "seems to enjoy taking failure and squeezing good from it."[3]

Find that hard to believe?

Consider the life of the apostle Paul. When people say to me, "God could never forgive me and use me after the way I've messed up," I tell them that they are not nearly as good at being bad as they think they are. Paul takes the honors, hands down, in the Best Sinner category. He refers to himself as a "blasphemer and a persecutor and a violent aggressor" (1 Timothy 1:13). Before his conversion, Paul regularly murdered men, women, and children in his sincere but misguided effort to extinguish Christianity.

And then Jesus Christ confronted Paul on the Damascus road—a confrontation that not only freed Paul from God's condemnation but began transforming him from chief sinner to chief spokesman for the Christian faith.

I thank Christ Jesus our Lord, who has strengthened me…putting me into service…. Yet for this reason I found mercy, so that in me as the foremost [sinner], Jesus Christ might demonstrate His perfect patience as an example for those who would believe in Him for eternal life. (1 Timothy 1:12, 16)

Before I became a Christian at age five, my biggest sins were stealing a friend's crayons and talking back to my mother. While those sins were certainly serious enough to condemn me, they didn't provide me with the credibility to travel the world saying, "If God can forgive me, He can forgive anyone." But Paul's tremendous failures qualified him to serve as Exhibit A of God's willingness to forgive everyone.

God's ability to transform our messes into successes continues today.

Charles Colson served as a special counsel to President Nixon. His political zeal led him to exclaim, "I would run over my grandmother to get Richard Nixon reelected." Yet his involvement in the Watergate cover-up led to disgrace and imprisonment. In his book *Born Again,* Colson describes how God used those catastrophic events to bring him to faith in Christ.

But Colson's conversion was not the end of the story; it was just the beginning.

The Divine Director was able to use Colson's mistakes in the first act of his life as the basis for an unbelievable second act. Being a former prisoner himself provided Colson with the platform to minister to hundreds of thousands of inmates and their families throughout the world. Colson explains the role that his biggest failure played in his most enduring success:

My life had been the perfect success story, the great American dream fulfilled. But all at once I realized that it was *not*
my success God had used to enable me to help those in this
prison, or in hundreds of others just like it. My life of success was not what made this morning so glorious—all my
achievements meant nothing in God's economy. No, the
real legacy of my life was my biggest failure—that I was
an ex-convict. My greatest humiliation—being sent to
prison—was the beginning of God's greatest use of my life;
He chose the one experience in which I could not glory for
His glory.[4]

Your greatest humiliation in life can set the stage for the greatest use of your life if you will follow the instructions of the Divine
Director.

However, before we discover how to do that, there's an important question we need to answer...

33

But Isn't the Script Already Written?

Almost as soon as the "I do's" were over, Missy Chadwick knew that her marriage to Brad was a mistake. After two years of constant bickering and brief extramarital affairs by each partner, Missy decided to end the relationship and start a new life with her eight-month-old daughter, Ashley.

Several months after the divorce was finalized, Missy met Steve Miller at a single-adult fellowship at her church. Three months later Missy and Steve were married. Although they have experienced normal marital ups and downs, the last thirteen years have been the happiest of Missy's life.

One day Ashley, now thirteen, asked her mom, "Was your marriage to my real dad a mistake?"

"Yes, honey, it was," Missy answered hesitantly, not knowing where the conversation was headed.

Ashley mused for a moment and then asked, "Then does that mean I was a mistake since I wouldn't have been born if you two hadn't gotten together?"

Missy didn't know how to respond to her daughter's question, because she didn't know the answer to her question.

• • •

Bill Sizemore faced similar confusion. Bill was "sucking fumes" financially, as they say in the oil business. His small energy-exploration company hadn't hit anything but dry holes for the last five years, and Bill had mortgaged everything he owned in search of the elusive find that could forever change his fortune.

One day a friend approached him with an offer to partner in drilling a wildcat well on a piece of property with a proven reserve of oil and natural gas. The cost for joining the partnership would be $100,000. The only unencumbered asset Bill had was a small well he'd inherited from his father that produced just enough revenue each month to keep Bill and his family solvent. That well's production was slowly diminishing, and Bill doubted it would provide enough collateral for a bank loan.

Not knowing what to do, Bill prayed for guidance: "God, if you want me to drill this well, give me a confirming sign."

The next day Bill went to the bank, showed the vice president all the production figures on his last remaining possession, and was surprised to hear, "We'll loan you up to $100,000 for your new venture."

To Bill, this was an obvious answer to prayer. He confidently gave the money to his new partner, and together they drilled... another dry hole.

Bill was devastated. Not just because he had lost his last asset, but because his faith in God's goodness—even His existence—was being tested. Bill had a number of unanswered questions: Why didn't God protect me from this mistake? Was this failure part of God's plan for my life, or was it beyond God's control? What point is there in serving a God who can't take care of me and answer my simple requests for guidance?

37

• • •

Missy's and Bill's stories raise interesting questions about God's role in our mistakes: If God's all-powerful and all-knowing (as He often claims in the Bible), then does His eternal plan include our mistakes? If our failures are part of God's plan, then how can we be held responsible? If God has already written the script for each of our lives, then does it really matter what we do—or don't do?

Obviously, these questions involve more than mere theological speculation. If we ever hope to recover from our failures and enjoy a second act in life, we must understand the role God plays in our mistakes.

I want to suggest four truths about God's role in our failures that at first may be difficult to swallow. However, before you close the book prematurely and conclude I'm out of my mind, I encourage you to finish the chapter and then decide for yourself.

GOD'S IN CONTROL

Perhaps you've heard the term "God's sovereignty" before and wondered what it means…and how it applies to you. The phrase refers to God's absolute rule over all His creation. "I am the LORD, and there is no other," God declares in Isaiah 45:6.

There aren't many forces controlling the universe—there's only one. And His name is Jehovah.

While many people agree with that statement in theory, they find it difficult to accept the practical ramifications of that truth.

Every time there's a great natural disaster, such as a tsunami, or a calamity, such as a terrorist attack, a secular radio show in New York enjoys calling me to get my perspective on the disaster, because they know it will light up the switchboard with irate callers.

"Whether or not God directly orchestrated the disaster, He's ultimately responsible for it," I say. "If God has the power to stop a catastrophe and doesn't, He has to be held accountable for its consequences."

Obviously, not everyone agrees with that conclusion!

"What about the laws of nature?" some people fire back.

"What about man's free will to make bad choices?"

"What about Satan's influence?" listeners howl in protest. "You can't hold God responsible for everything that happens in the world."

38

They have a point. Many of the problems in the world are directly attributable to human foibles, some are the result of natural forces, and even a few can be directly linked to Satan and his sinister forces of darkness. But ultimately, either God is in control of His creation, or He isn't. One cannot be semisovereign any more than a woman can be semipregnant.

God's absolute reign over His creation includes His control of Satan, who led a heavenly revolt against the Creator (as Martin Luther said, "The devil is God's devil"); Adam and Eve, whose disobedience alienated mankind from God; the nation of Israel as it repeatedly rebelled against God's Law; and even the Jewish and Roman leaders who nailed the Son of God to a cross. None of these individual choices to rebel against God diminished His control in the slightest.

If God is in control of everything that happens in His creation, then *everything* also includes your mistakes.

Your divorce, your failed business venture, your lapse of morality, your missed opportunities, or your poor choices may result in some painful consequences, but they do not loosen God's grip on the direction of your life. God is still in control.

Your failure is no match for God's sovereignty.

GOD HAS A PLAN FOR YOU

I'm continually amazed at the number of people who argue with the idea that God has a detailed master plan that governs our lives. They picture God as passively watching and waiting for us to make our choices as free human agents and then adjusting His plan to fit our preferences.

Do we really believe God would surrender control of His creation to the whims of His creatures? Is it plausible that a universe so intricate in design is run by Someone whose motto is "The best ability is flexibility" when it comes to planning?

My former pastor Dr. W. A. Criswell once observed:

> Before a stone was laid in the construction of St. Paul's
> Cathedral in London, the idea was born in the mind of
> Sir Christopher Wren. He saw it in his mind and purposed
> it in his heart. Before he struck a chisel against the heavy
> rock of marble, Michelangelo saw the mighty Moses in his
> mind and purposed it in his heart.... Why should it sur-
> prise us then that God, the designer and architect of the
> universe, should have a plan and purpose for His creation?
> The greater the project, the more necessary the plan.[1]

God has a detailed plan for the universe that governs everything that happens in His creation. The apostle Paul described that plan when he wrote,

> Also we have obtained an inheritance, having been predes-
> tined according to His purpose who works *all things* after
> the counsel of His will. (Ephesians 1:11, emphasis added)

"All things" fall within God's intricate design for His creation. "All things" also encompasses everything that might affect your life.

Your circumstances. The decisions of governmental leaders (Proverbs 21:1), the outcome of the rolled dice in a Las Vegas casino (Proverbs 16:33), and the change of seasons (Daniel 2:21, NIV) are just some of the external circumstances that God directs. Obviously, each of these forces has the power to impact your life.

Your physical and emotional makeup. "All things" also includes the smallest details of your life. The color of your eyes, the number of hairs on your head, and even the bent of your emotions were all designed by God. The psalmist expressed that truth this way:

41

> For You formed my inward parts;
> You wove me in my mother's womb.
> I will give thanks to You, for I am fearfully and wonderfully
> made;
> Wonderful are Your works,
> And my soul knows it very well. (Psalm 139:13–14)

Your choices. God's design for your life not only includes those circumstances beyond your control but also those parts of your life that you assume are under your control. You may think you're in charge of how you spend your time, the route you drive to work, the items you purchase at the supermarket, or even whether you finish reading this book. But consider what the writer of Proverbs claims:

> Man's steps are ordained by the LORD,
> How then can man understand his way? (Proverbs 20:24)

Every step we take has been planned by God? I agree with the writer that such a thought is beyond comprehension. Yet it only makes sense that God would exercise control over the most minute details of our lives if His overall plan is to be accomplished.

For example, if every part of your physical makeup was determined by God, then that means there was only one man and one woman whose genetics could have produced you. Therefore, God had to orchestrate the events surrounding your mother's and father's births so they were born during the same period in history. He had to move them to exactly the right geographical location so they would meet one another. He also had to ensure that they were sufficiently attracted to each other (at just the right time) to conceive you. It's mind-blowing when you think about it!

God's intricate plan governing your choices is not only logical; it is also biblical. Read the psalmist's words carefully:

And in Your book were all written
The days that were ordained for me,
When as yet there was not one of them. (Psalm 139:16)

God not only planned the number of days you would have on earth but also how you would spend those days. Your life span and your activities are inseparably linked to each other. What you eat, whether or not you exercise, where you live, the doctors you visit (or don't), and a thousand other choices you make each day play a large part in determining the number of days you spend on planet Earth.

One Thursday afternoon a few years ago, I left work a few

minutes early for a haircut. On the way to the barbershop, I passed through an intersection and within a few seconds heard a screeching of brakes. I glanced in my rearview mirror and saw the car behind me decimated by another vehicle running a red light. I pulled off to the side of the road and dialed 911, but it was too late.

The driver was dead.

Later that evening I couldn't help but reflect on what had happened. What if I'd left work only a few seconds later? What if the pressure I'd applied to the accelerator had been just a little bit lighter? What if the driver who ran the red light had been applying a little more pressure to his accelerator?

My life could have been snuffed out in an instant that day.

No, I'm not implying that God loved me more than He did the victim of the accident. What I am suggesting is that since the day of my birth and the day of my death are written on God's calendar, He must have a detailed plan that includes every aspect of my life, including my choices.

Your failures. If all your steps are directed by God, wouldn't that include your missteps and stumbles? That only makes sense. The story line of your life—already written by the Divine Author— includes all your choices, not just the good ones. Since the psalmist used our birth as an example of God's intricate plan for every aspect of our lives, let's continue using that analogy for a moment.

What if your conception was the result of the premarital liaison of two hormonally charged teenagers, an extramarital affair, or even a rape? Such conceptions occur every hour of every day.

After reading Psalm 139, could you really say your birth was an accident?

43

Somehow God was able to use the moral failure of others to accomplish His plan for you. If God can use other people's mistakes for good, why are we surprised that He can also use our mistakes to achieve His purpose? It's a mind-boggling thought!

GOD CAN ACCOMPLISH HIS PLAN
FOR YOUR LIFE

Perhaps you agree with everything you've read up to this point. You believe in an all-powerful God who rules over the universe. You accept that God has a detailed plan encompassing every part of your life. *But don't we, other people, or Satan occasionally alter God's preferred plan for our life?* we wonder. That question has led some people to conclude that God actually has two wills: His perfect will and His permissive will (think of them as Plan A and Plan B).

According to this theory, God's perfect will includes what God wishes would happen, but His permissive will is what actually happens. When you ask people for examples of God's permissive will, they will usually cite all the problems in the world for which there are no easy answers: starving babies, devastating floods, undeserved suffering. "God hates these things as much as we do. He would love to prevent them, but the laws of nature or man's free will prevent God from intervening," we are told.

But do we really believe that God has been handcuffed by His own laws or by His own creatures so that He is incapable of executing His preferred plan? While the concept of God's having a Plan A and Plan B may seem logical, it is completely unbiblical.

Nowhere in the Bible do we find the concept of God's having two wills. Instead, God's Word says that He "works all things after the counsel of His *will* [singular, not plural]" (Ephesians 1:11, emphasis added).

Remember, God is not semisovereign. The benefit of being the King is that you never have to settle for second best. There is only one will that determines what ultimately happens in the universe, and it is God's will.

The Old Testament character Job had reason to question God's control over the world, especially when Job's world seemed to be spinning out of control. In a short period of time, Job lost his children, his possessions, and his health. Some of Job's friends tried the two-wills theory to explain what was happening to him. In essence, they argued that Job missed out on God's perfect will because of his own sin. But Job arrived at a different conclusion (with a little help from the Almighty) about God's absolute control over all His creation:

I know that You can do all things,
And that no purpose of Yours can be thwarted. (Job 42:2)

Job was saying, "God, I don't pretend to understand what You are up to in my life. But I believe that You have a plan, even though, in this blizzard of calamities, I can't see what that plan is."

I can already hear you shouting back your objections. "But what about my responsibility for my actions? If what you are saying is true, then we are simply robots with no control over our destinies.

Why even bother to get up in the morning if everything in my life has already been determined?"

GOD'S SOVEREIGNTY DOES NOT EXEMPT
YOU FROM RESPONSIBILITY

God's detailed plan for your life—a plan that even includes your failures—doesn't mean you're not responsible for your actions. How can we possibly reconcile God's absolute power over our choices with our responsibility for those choices?

We still must make wise choices. A young man came to the late Bible teacher J. Vernon McGee and said, "Dr. McGee, I've been studying predestination, and I'm so convinced of the sovereignty of God that I believe if I stood in the middle of a busy highway, and my hour had not yet come, God would spare my life."

Dr. McGee, responding with his characteristic wit, said, "Son, if you stand in the middle of a busy highway, your hour has come."

God's control over our lives doesn't negate our responsibility to exercise good judgment in our decisions. As Solomon counseled, "He who trusts in his own heart is a fool, but he who walks wisely will be delivered [from oncoming traffic!]" (Proverbs 28:26).

We still suffer the natural consequences of our actions and decisions. The fact that our failures are included in God's plan for our lives does not prevent us from suffering the consequences of those failures.

Think for a moment about Jesus's death on the cross. Certainly Christ's death was no accident. God determined before the beginning of time that He would send His Son to die for the sins of the world. Nevertheless, God used the wrong choices of two leaders—Herod Antipas and Pontius Pilate—to accomplish His purpose.

> For Herod Antipas, Pontius Pilate the governor, the Gentiles, and the people of Israel were all united against Jesus, your holy servant, whom you anointed. But everything they did was determined beforehand according to your will. (Acts 4:27–28, NLT)

47

Although Herod's and Pilate's actions against Christ were part of God's elaborate plan to accomplish the redemption of mankind, these two men still had to suffer the eternal consequences of their decisions.

Similarly, we may have to experience the fallout from divorces, affairs, terminations, and financial mistakes even though they were included in God's master plan for our lives.

Admittedly, there are difficult questions for which there are no easy answers. How can we be responsible for our failures if those failures are part of God's plan for our lives? How can we reconcile God's sovereignty with our responsibility? The honest answer is "I don't know—and neither does anyone else."

Perhaps this illustration will help. If you've ever been on a cruise, you know that during your time on the ship, you're constantly making choices: where to dine, whether to stay up for the midnight buffet, what entertainment to enjoy, whether to play shuffleboard or sit by the pool. Yet, in spite of these choices you make on the ship, your destination has already been determined and is under the control of the captain.

In the same way, we make decisions each day that appear to be our choice. Nevertheless, our lives are still under the control of the Captain, who has already determined our ultimate destination.

But even that illustration is lacking. Ultimately, it's impossible for our finite minds to grasp the workings of an infinite God. One person wisely observed: "Try to explain predestination, and you will lose your mind. Try to explain it away, and you may lose your soul."

GOD'S SOVEREIGNTY OFFERS PEACE FROM YOUR PAST, HOPE FOR YOUR FUTURE

Too often the truths we have discussed so far are viewed negatively. God's control over our lives means that we are nothing but puppets, we assume. Our responsibility for our actions means that we must remain prisoners of our mistakes, we fear. But these twin truths of God's sovereignty and our responsibility for our actions actually offer great hope for those of us who have failed miserably.

God's sovereignty means that our blowups don't mess up His plan for us. My friend Chuck Swindoll says it much more eloquently:

When a man or woman of God fails, nothing of God fails. When a man or woman of God changes, nothing of God changes. When someone dies, nothing of God dies. When our lives are altered by the unexpected, nothing of God is altered or unexpected.[2]

However, the fact that our actions have consequences also offers great hope for our future. God has given us the freedom to make choices that can positively affect the direction of our lives. Personal failures and catastrophes can actually be catalysts for changes in us that produce a brighter future for us.

The great entrepreneur J. C. Penney experienced more than his share of failures and mishaps and learned how these truths work in real life. In 1898, he went to work for Guy Johnson and Thomas Callahan, who operated some small dry-goods stores called Golden Rule Stores. Because of his tirelessness and high ethical and moral standards, he succeeded to the point of eventually buying out Johnson and Callahan and renaming the chain of stores.

Then in 1910, Penney's wife died, and at a friend's suggestion, Penney turned to philanthropy as a way to deal with his pain. In 1916, he met his second wife, but eight years later she suddenly died also. Penney married a third time, poured his life into his work, and by 1929 accumulated a net worth of $40 million. Then the Great Depression wiped out all his wealth.

Devastated emotionally and physically, Penney entered a sanitarium in Battle Creek, Michigan. As he lay in bed one day, he heard a familiar hymn from the chapel. The doctors didn't expect him to live, but Penney decided he wasn't yet ready to give up. He cried out to God for help, and the Lord answered his request. Penney later said that immediately his depression was lifted, and soon he left the sanitarium.

Once again he built his great fortune and further established the company we know today as JCPenney. For decades, he gave away millions of dollars and shared his faith in God with anyone who would listen. At age ninety, Penney was still enjoying his second act in life; he believed not only in God's power but in his own ability to affect his future through wise choices. J. C. Penney made the decision not to allow his failure to become his finale.[3]

How do we reconcile our responsibility for our failures with God's sovereignty over our failures?

General Robert E. Lee, the leader of the Confederate forces during the Civil War, offers some helpful insight to that question. After his defeat, Lee became president of Washington College and sought to train men to help rebuild a nation that had been torn apart. One day Lee asked a student who was not performing satisfactorily to come to his office. Lee admonished him about the importance of hard work to experience success in life. The student responded, "But, General, you failed."

Instead of rebuking the student, Lee said, "I hope that you may be more fortunate than I." He then elaborated to a friend, "We failed, but in the good providence of God, apparent failure often proves a blessing."[4]

Failures can be transformed into successes, but the transformation doesn't occur automatically. In the pages that follow, we will discover God's five principles for turning your biggest messes into incredible successes.

ACT 2

Turning
Your
Messes
into
Successes

FESS UP TO
YOUR MESS-UP

L ife's filled with perplexing questions for which there seem to
be no easy answers. For example...

Why isn't *phonics* spelled the way it sounds?

Why are there interstate highways in Hawaii?

If a vegetarian eats only vegetables, what does a humanitarian
eat?

If someone with a multiple-personality disorder threatens to
commit suicide, is that a hostage situation?

If you throw a cat out the window, is that kitty litter?

You've seen those virtually indestructible flight-recorder boxes
that are discovered among the smoldering remains of a crashed airplane. Why don't they build the whole airplane out of that material?

Here's one more: Why do we instinctively deny our failures

rather than admit them? You would think we would eventually learn that covering up our mistakes never works. But that doesn't keep us from trying, does it?

As I write these words, a top government official in Washington DC is embroiled in yet another scandal. The special prosecutor was not able to charge the official with a crime, but he has accused him of lying to cover up an alleged crime that turned out not to be a crime. (Only in Washington would that make sense.)

Last night I heard a veteran television reporter observe, "It's the same story since the Watergate fiasco. It's not the crime that ends up getting you but the cover-up of the crime."

Actually, the tendency to hide our failures predates Watergate. It all started with Edengate. After Adam and Eve disobeyed God, they automatically felt guilty and tried to cover up their guilt with some ill-fitting fig leaves. A cool breeze in the garden made the first couple aware of the inadequacy of their custom-made garments ("Eve, do you feel a draft in here?"), causing them to hide when they heard God approaching. They knew from the tone of His voice that He wasn't in a particularly good mood.

As Ricky Ricardo used to say to Lucy, God said, *Adam, you've got some 'splaining to do!* Without thinking twice, Adam in one simple sentence laid his failure at the feet of both God and Eve: "It was the woman you gave me who gave me the fruit, and I ate it" (Genesis 3:12, NLT).

Jeffress paraphrase: "I was perfectly happy communing with the fruit flies and the hippopotamuses, but noooooo, You had to stick me with this woman. Don't blame me—blame her."

So God turns to the woman and asks for an explanation. Hav-

54

ing caught on quickly to this new sport called the blame game, she responds, "I was having my daily quiet time thinking about how much I love You, God, when out of nowhere this serpent—that You created—made me an offer I couldn't refuse."

Since that episode in Eden, we've all become rather adept at the same sport. When we fail, our first instinct is to cover it up and hope no one notices. When we are exposed, our first impulse is to accuse others and hope everyone agrees.

Failing to accept responsibility for our failures prevents us from receiving the forgiveness we desperately need, and it also precludes us from experiencing the new beginning we desperately desire. Pastor and author Gordon MacDonald, who openly admitted his own moral failure many years ago, reminds us that God doesn't automatically turn our messes into successes:

> Failures are transformed—or not—depending on the state of our hearts. Some people drench failure with clever euphemisms, wiggle out of responsibility, circumvent consequences and scatter blame with panicked liberality. God requires a radically different response to failure: Failures must be named; consequences accepted.[1]

The first and perhaps most important decision we have to make about our failures is whether we're willing to "fess up to our mess-up." I'll admit, it isn't easy to accept responsibility for our blowups. Denial is more than a river in Egypt—it's a way of living for most of us, especially when it comes to mistakes.

So why do we find it so hard to admit we've blown it?

Why We Deny

There are at least three reasons we find it difficult to admit our failures.

Pride. A few months ago my wife, her sister, and I were driving back from a restaurant where we'd celebrated my in-laws' fiftieth wedding anniversary. I hadn't listened as carefully as I should have to the directions for getting back to the cabin where we were staying and suddenly found myself driving along an unfamiliar path.

You ladies can probably write the rest of this story.

Instead of stopping and asking for directions, I kept traveling in the wrong direction, reasoning to myself that eventually I would arrive in the right place (which is technically true, if I didn't mind a side trip through China).

Pride prevented me from admitting my mistake and receiving the needed assistance.

The essence of pride is an inflated view of self; it's an issue of convincing ourselves that we're not like other mortals. We think more highly of ourselves than we should, as Paul warns against in Romans 12:3.

The result is, when we experience failure, we want to blame someone else for our problem. Divorces, terminations, or financial mishaps must be someone else's fault, we instinctively assume.

Other times our pride causes us to gloss over our mistakes. We treat our mistakes as inconsequential when compared to our perceived greatness. On one occasion, Winston Churchill demonstrated this when he was arguing with one of his servants:

"You were rude," Churchill charged.

His servant replied, "You were rude too."

"Yes," Churchill grumbled, "but I am a great man."[2]

Pride can cause us to automatically deny or too easily dismiss our mistakes. Sometimes pride itself is the primary cause of our failure.

A wife convinces herself that a friendship with another man is safe because she is too moral to ever fall into an affair.

A pastor launches into a new building program that the majority of the church opposes, because he is convinced he is more connected to God than his parishioners.

A worker close to retirement invests his entire nest egg in a "can't-miss stock" because he's sure he is more financially astute than his wife, who voices concern.

Fear. At other times we allow fear to keep us from acknowledging mistakes. We're afraid that admitting our failure will result in a painful loss:

- Admitting a poor decision at work will result in the loss of our job.
- Admitting a broken confidence will result in the loss of a friendship.
- Admitting an affair will result in the loss of our marriage.
- Admitting an addiction will result in the loss of respect of those we care about.

Fear was the major motivation for Adam and Eve's ineffective, vegetative cover-up. "I was afraid" was Adam's explanation for attempting to hide his failure from God.

I wish I could say that, when we fail, we have nothing to fear

57

but fear itself. It would be nice to be able to promise that, if you simply admit your mistake, everyone will applaud your honesty and automatically forgive your failure.

But you know better.

Those who admit their failures often experience painful consequences such as divorce, humiliation, termination, and imprisonment. Confession does not always (or even frequently) result in acquittal.

I believe Adam instinctively understood that truth. He wanted to postpone his day of reckoning as long as possible, because he realized that his failure would result in very painful consequences. Even if God forgave the first couple (which He did), they would still have to experience the fallout of their mistake, and that ultimately included:

- banishment from their home in the garden (this is the first incident of moving—and therefore the first mention of hell—in the Bible)
- pain in childbirth (no epidurals for Eve)
- difficulty in work (lots of blood, sweat, and tears for Adam and the rest of us)

What person in his right mind wouldn't try to deny his failure as long as possible, which leads to a third reason we find it difficult to admit our mistakes.

Ignorance. We try to hide our mistakes because we naively believe we *can* hide them. Even though we regularly witness other people's mistakes being exposed, we've convinced ourselves that we are better cover-up artists than they are. Unfortunately, we're like the little boy who vehemently denies he was anywhere close to the cookie jar even though the crumbs are dangling from his mouth as he speaks.

No matter how hard you try to hide the evidence, sooner or later your failures are going to be known to others. Remember the story of King Saul from the Old Testament? Although God had commanded Saul to destroy the Amalekites and everything they had, Saul thought that was a little extreme. Why kill perfectly good sheep and oxen that he could put to profitable use?

59

Speaking of profit, when the prophet Samuel confronted Saul about his disobedience to God, the king refused to own up to his mistake. "I've followed God's command completely and destroyed everything!" he claimed. Samuel might have been tempted to believe him were it not for the crumbs dangling from Saul's mouth...or more precisely, the sounds of stolen sheep and oxen that were drowning out Saul's protest of innocence.

> But Samuel said, "What then is this bleating of the sheep
> in my ears, and the lowing of the oxen which I hear?"
> (1 Samuel 15:14)

The problem with covering up our failures is that failures refuse to be covered up. Eventually the sheep will bleat, the crumbs will become visible, and our failure will be exposed.

Confession Is Good for the Soul

But beyond the ineffectiveness of cover-ups, there are at least four positive reasons for admitting rather than denying our mistakes.

1. Admitting Failure Allows Us to Receive God's Forgiveness

Augustine said, "God only gives to those whose hands are empty." Only when we are ready to empty ourselves of denials and rationalizations for our failures will we be in a position to receive God's forgiveness for our mistakes. As we saw in chapter 2, God's more than willing to forgive…but we must be willing to ask.

May I share a secret with you? God already knows about your failures. He's aware of

- your addiction,
- your bankruptcy,
- your divorce,
- your immorality,
- your squandered opportunities.

But He can't forgive you as long as you're trying to forgive yourself by excusing, denying, or blaming others for your failures. Aren't you ready to take off those ill-fitting fig leaves and ask God to cover your failures with His forgiveness?

2. Admitting Failure Renews Our Emotional and Physical Vitality

Nothing can sap your emotional and physical strength more than lingering guilt over unconfessed mistakes. Research shows a relationship between the acknowledgment of failure and physical health.

Author Timothy Jones notes recent studies that have demonstrated that people who admit to failure and who openly discuss their foibles experience both short-term and long-term health benefits. According to researcher James Pennebaker, "There appears to be within us something akin to an urge to confess. Not disclosing our thoughts and feelings can be unhealthy. Disclosing them can be healthy."[3]

King David experienced the physical and emotional downside of denial after his moral failure with Bathsheba. As David reflected on the months he spent covering over his failure, he wrote:

When I kept silent about my sin, my body wasted away
Through my groaning all day long.
For day and night Your hand was heavy upon me;
My vitality was drained away as with the fever heat of
       summer. (Psalm 32:3–4)

However, once David admitted his failure, he experienced immediate relief:

I acknowledged my sin to You,
And my iniquity I did not hide;
I said, "I will confess my transgressions to the LORD";
And You forgave the guilt of my sin....

Be glad in the LORD and rejoice, you righteous ones,
And shout for joy, all you who are upright in heart.
       (Psalm 32:5, 11)

Are you physically and emotionally exhausted from trying to hide your mistakes? Are you tired of worrying day and night what will happen when others discover your failure? Nothing compares to the relief that comes from the knowledge that your mistake has been forgiven. But that forgiveness can be received only with empty hands.

3. Admitting Failure Encourages Us to Move On

One morning recently I stepped out of the shower ready to dry my hair. After plugging the hair dryer into the outlet, I flipped the On switch and…nothing. I clicked it several more times, illustrating the definition of a moron: someone who does the same thing repeatedly, expecting different results. Finally I reached over and pressed the small, red Reset button in the plug, and the dryer began to blow.

Occasionally it helps to hit the emotional Reset button in our lives. We need to start over and head in a new direction. Admitting to God, to others, and to ourselves that we have blown it helps us make a clear delineation between the past and the future. Our acknowledgment of failure serves as a marker for the beginning of our second act. Whenever we're haunted by guilt over our failure or we're tempted to repeat the same mistake, we can say, "Since that is part of my past and not part of my future, I'm not going there again."

Remember the story from chapter 2 about the youth minister who was caught in an inappropriate relationship with a student, was fired from his job, and considered taking his own life? Eventually Carlo Walth admitted his failure, accepted God's forgiveness, received extensive counseling, and was restored to a place of ministry. But the key to his new beginning was a willingness to admit his failure:

I'll never forget the night I first told my daughters (age 5 and 7 at that time) that "daddy had made some big mistakes and that we wouldn't be able to go back to our church anymore." They were sad, but when I told them that from then on, every night would be a family night, they jumped up and danced around waving their arms crying "Yeah!"

In a very dark time, God touched me with the unique perspective of my kids. There was a point when I thought that if people knew where I was coming from, I'd never be able to serve in a church again. But the fact that my testimony has been completely up front has made a very large positive difference in my life and ministry.[4]

Carlo Walth found the Reset button for his life that allowed him to experience a fresh beginning. It was labeled Confession.

4. Admitting Failure Allows Us to Learn from Mistakes

Someone has used the word *mistake* as an acrostic for the benefits of failure. Mistakes are...

Messages that give us feedback about life;
Interruptions that should cause us to reflect and
    think;
Signposts that direct us to the right path;
Tests that push us toward greater maturity;
Awakenings that keep us in the game mentally;

> **K**eys that we can use to unlock the next door of
> opportunity;
> **E**xplorations that let us journey where we've never
> been before;
> **S**tatements about our development and progress.[5]

However, each of those statements represents only a potential benefit of failure. If we are unwilling to label an episode in our lives as a failure, we will never be free to learn from our mistake. For example, Thomas Edison is often quoted as saying that he learned ten thousand ways not to make a light bulb before he discovered one way to make a light bulb.

But inside that humorous quip is a serious but simple truth: until we're willing to admit our failure, we cannot profit from our failure.

My grandfather was financially astute. To my knowledge, he never borrowed any money. I can still hear him saying, "Robert, interest can either be your greatest friend or your greatest enemy. It either works for you or against you."

The same can be said about mistakes.

The first step in making your mistakes work for you rather than against you is to admit that you've made a mistake.

HOW TO FESS UP

Now that we've discovered the benefits of admitting our failures, how do we do so in a positive and healthy way?

1. Determine If You've Really Failed

John Ortberg correctly observes that "failure is not an event, but rather a judgment about an event. Failure is not something that happens to us or a label we attach to things. It's a way we think about outcomes."[6]

Stop for a moment and reread the previous paragraph slowly. What we sometimes call a failure is simply our subjective judgment about an event at a point in time.

For example, my family has not yet entered the era of digital photography. We still take snapshots, develop them, and paste them in a photo book. I can look back in our picture album from six years ago and see a photograph of one of my daughters when she was eight. Although the snapshot accurately represents her at that point in time, it bears little resemblance to her appearance today as a teenager.

Suppose someone other than her loving dad looked at that picture and said, "Boy, that girl is a little hefty. She needs to lose some weight."

The problem with such a judgment is that it's based on a subjective standard (the proper weight for an eight-year-old is debatable). More important, the judgment is based on a picture that is six years old. Anyone who saw my daughter today wouldn't encourage her to lose an ounce.

Before you (or others) label an event in your life as a failure, you need to ask yourself two important questions:

What standard am I using to make my judgment?

Sometimes an unrealistic standard leads us to the faulty

conclusion we have failed. For example, someone who opens a small retail store and is distraught because he doesn't have the same sales volume as the local Wal-Mart has based his judgment on an unrealistic expectation. Instead of using a superconglomerate as the basis of comparison, he should look at the results of a similar-sized store in a similar-sized town. Of course, some areas of life have no absolute standards for success, which is why the Bible warns against comparing ourselves to others. To judge your marriage, your children, your career, or the totality of your life as a failure is often a mistake, because doing so fails to recognize the unique plan God has for you.

Am I making this judgment prematurely?

Like Thomas Edison, Jonas Salk was an inventor who understood the value of mistakes. Before Salk developed a vaccine for polio that actually worked, he discovered two hundred that didn't. Someone asked him, "How did it feel to fail two hundred times?" Salk replied, "I never failed two hundred times in my life. I was taught not to use the word *failure*. I just discovered two hundred ways how not to vaccinate for polio."[7]

Just because your children rebel against your authority now doesn't mean they'll never listen to you.

Just because you didn't receive the desired promotion this year doesn't mean you won't get it next year.

Just because you lost a significant amount of money in the stock market over the last five years doesn't mean you will lose money next year.

Just because your relationship with God isn't as intimate as it has been in the past doesn't mean it won't improve in the future.

66

Remember, failure is like a snapshot. It's a judgment about an event, based on a subjective standard, and made at a point in time. Failure is not always final.

2. Identify the Role Others Have Played

If we're going to learn from our mistakes, we must objectively acknowledge what role—if any—others may have played in our failures. Divorces, bankruptcies, financial setbacks, terminations, and lapses of morality are rarely our fault exclusively. While refusing to focus on the part others may have played in our failure may seem like the Christian thing to do, it's, in fact, a dumb thing to do for several reasons.

First, failing to identify how others may have contributed to our failure may cause us to fall into the failure trap again. A woman who blames only herself for a divorce from an abusive husband is in danger of marrying the same kind of man again. The small-business owner who denies the role a dishonest partner played in a failed venture may choose a similar partner again.

Additionally, failing to identify the role others have played in our failure prevents us from experiencing the healing effects of forgiveness. For the last week I've battled an infection. I tried ignoring it, because I didn't have time to go to the doctor. I hoped the infection would heal itself. But it didn't. Eventually the discomfort, sluggishness, and high fever forced me to see my physician and take the necessary antibiotics to clear the infection. Today I feel energized and ready to take on the world.

Bitterness is an infection of the soul. No matter how successful we are in temporarily ignoring the sickness, it eventually will poison our entire being unless we treat it with the antibiotic known as forgiveness.

Before we have the freedom to begin a second act in life, we must forgive those who played a role in our first-act failure. And we can only forgive those whom we're willing to blame.

Forgiveness is not denying someone wronged us. Forgiveness is acknowledging someone injured us and then releasing our right to hurt our offender for hurting us. As the late Lewis Smedes said, "When we genuinely forgive, we set a prisoner free and then discover that the prisoner we set free was us."[8]

3. Acknowledge Your Responsibility

Even if the failure you have experienced is 99 percent someone else's fault, you still need to fess up to your 1 percent of responsibility.

Why is that so important?

First, as we saw in the last section, we can never learn from our failure if we're unwilling to admit our part in the failure. For example, why is the probability of divorce greater for second marriages than for first marriages? I believe it's because many refuse to admit the role they played in their first marital failure, dooming themselves to repeat the same mistake.

A well-known ministerial colleague of mine went through a very public divorce. People excused his divorce saying, "His wife was emotionally unstable." Every time my wife, Amy, hears that, she asks, "But who made her that way?" We must acknowledge whatever part we played in our failure if we're going to enjoy a second act in life.

Second, admitting our failure may encourage other people to

help us. Imagine that two friends come to you on the same day and ask for financial assistance.

The first one says, "Would you lend me five hundred dollars? I don't know how I got in the shape I'm in. Bad luck, I suppose."

The second friend says, "Would you lend me five hundred dollars? I made a mistake and used my credit card too often. But I've learned my lesson and cut my Visa card in half."

Which friend would you be more inclined to help?

God isn't the only one who "is opposed to the proud, but gives grace to the humble" (1 Peter 5:5). Because we're created in His image, we're also naturally inclined to be more sympathetic with those who admit their faults than with those who deny them.

So to whom should we fess up when we fail?

If our failure is personal and hasn't injured another person or offended God, we need only to admit the failure to ourselves. For example, occasionally (or frequently, depending on whom you talk with) I deliver a less-than-spectacular sermon on Sunday morning. Even though I may have taught God's Word accurately, I feel something was missing. The sermon could have been shorter, or maybe I should have used a different closing illustration, or possibly the message should have been structured differently.

I've committed no sin that needs to be confessed to God, nor have I hurt the congregation substantially—they still received a message from God's Word. But I acknowledge to myself that I could have done better—and then I go take a nap.

However, if our failure has injured another person, we need to seek forgiveness from that person.

When you ask someone for forgiveness, never focus on what

he or she may have done wrong, but instead acknowledge your failure. An apology that begins "I realize both of us are to blame for this problem, but since I'm a better person than you are, I'm making the first move by asking your forgiveness for whatever part I may have played in this problem" is sure to be met with a cool reception.

Remember, the other person is already aware of what you've done wrong. He wants to know if you are aware.

Whether or not another person chooses to forgive you for your failure is often beyond your control. However, admitting your mistake and seeking forgiveness allows you to experience a clear conscience.

Someone has defined a clear conscience as the confidence that no one can accuse you of a wrong you have not attempted to make right. Such confidence is vital to launching a second act in life.

4. Receive God's Forgiveness

Whether or not others choose to forgive your failure, God is willing to forgive…if you're willing to ask. But enough of the theoretical. It's time to take advantage of God's offer—because a gift that's never received isn't a gift at all.

The first step to launching a new beginning in your life is to receive God's forgiveness for your mistake. Are you ready to empty your hands of the bitterness, denials, or rationalizations that you've held on to in order to justify your failure?

Remember, God gives only to those who approach Him with empty hands.

May I suggest that you stop right now, close your eyes, and say something like this to God:

Heavenly Father, I know I have failed and failed miserably. I am truly sorry for the way I have disappointed You. I believe that You sent Your Son, Jesus Christ, to die on the cross for my failures. Right now I'm asking You to forgive me, not because I deserve to be forgiven, but because Christ has already paid for my mistakes. Now that You have forgiven me, I ask You for the opportunity to start over. Thank You for being a God who gives second chances. In Jesus's name, amen.

However, even though God may choose to forgive and forget our mistakes, it's important that we do something else with our failures before we completely forget about them...

Don't Mess Up
for Free

For three decades Woody Allen was a Hollywood superstar-director. His films, including the Academy Award–winning *Annie Hall,* grossed tens of millions of dollars and allowed him complete artistic freedom to pursue whatever projects he chose.

Then in 1992, Allen's girlfriend, Mia Farrow, discovered nude photographs he had taken of Farrow's adopted daughter, who was twenty-one at the time.

Allen admitted to having an affair with the young woman, whom he later married. The resulting scandal caused public opinion to turn viciously against Allen.

Today, Woody Allen's films attract only a minuscule audience in America. The once sought-after director has found it difficult to convince any major film studio to finance his projects. He's lost millions of dollars in lawsuits defending himself against charges of child abuse involving Mia Farrow's other children.

Perhaps the greatest tragedy of all is that Woody Allen has learned nothing from his failures. In a recent interview in *Vanity Fair,* he confessed, "I've gained no wisdom, no insight, no mellowing. I would make all the same mistakes again, today."[1]

Hollywood moguls are not the only ones who fail to learn from their failures. Every day of the week ordinary people choose to repeat their mistakes rather than learn from them:

- A woman in an abusive marriage finally ends the relationship, only to choose another man just like the one she divorced.

- An investor bets the ranch on a highly speculative venture and loses everything, only to repeat the mistake as soon as he emerges from bankruptcy.

- An employee is dismissed after the discovery of his inflated résumé, only to lie again in order to secure another position.

- A husband whose addiction to Internet pornography almost costs him his marriage spends months in counseling, only to return to the computer screen as soon as he completes his therapy.

Remember, failure is inevitable. In addition to the smaller financial, relational, and spiritual mistakes that plague us regularly, we're going to make some gigantic blunders that will bring catastrophic results into our lives: termination, bankruptcy, divorce, and humiliation.

Although God's grace can exempt us from the eternal conse-quences of our failure, rarely does God's forgiveness remove the temporary pain we must experience because of our mistakes.

Simply put, you're going to pay a price for your failure. You may pay in one lump sum or in monthly installments, but your failure is going to cost you something. By the way, the fact that God usually requires you to experience the pain of your failure is a sign of God's love, not His hatred for you.

For example, a rancher who erects an electric or barbed-wire fence around his acreage does so to protect his cattle. Even though the animal may experience a shock or sting when it attempts to move beyond the established boundary, the momentary pain keeps it from wandering onto a busy road or into the hands of a rustler.

But it still hurts!

Similarly, God allows those of us who are "the sheep of His pasture" to experience the pain of our failures to encourage us to live within His boundaries.

Profiting from Your Failure

Failure can exact a heavy toll on our lives. Although we have no choice about paying the price of our failure, we can choose whether we want to continue paying the cost or learn from our mistakes.

Imagine your house undergoing foundation problems. Doors that don't close and plaster cracks along the ceiling convince you that something is wrong. Not knowing what to do, you pay a foundation expert two hundred dollars to evaluate your home. He informs you that although your house is in the beginning stages of a serious problem, you can prevent further shifting by regularly watering around the perimeter of your house.

You pay the consultant his fee but decide that watering is too time-consuming and costly, so you ignore his advice.

Six months later your home develops serious problems that require ten thousand dollars of repair work.

76

Why would you pay for advice then ignore it?

Yet we make a similar mistake if we ignore the invaluable counsel we automatically purchase when we fail. Instead of viewing our mistakes—and their consequences—as unwelcome circumstances over which we have no control, what if we could think of failure as a highly paid consultant hired to help us plan the rest of our lives?

When I turned forty, I hired a consultant to spend a day with my wife and me to help us plan the next several decades of our lives with a special focus on our ministry. His fee for one day was three thousand dollars. After shelling out that kind of money, do you think I stared out the window, daydreaming about what I was going to order for lunch?

No, I was listening carefully, and more than a decade later I still pore over the copious notes I took that day, trying to wring every ounce of value from the counsel that cost me so many dollars!

Similarly, you have probably already paid a steep price for your failure. You can spend the rest of your life lamenting the unfair price, or you can view your failure as an expensive consultant hired to give you important guidance about your future.

You can still choose to ignore the advice your failure offers, or you can learn from it. Since the failure fee is nonrefundable, why not choose the latter?

The Bible uses the term *reproof* to describe the lessons that failure provides. A reproof is a negative consequence that results from a mistake. Sometimes that negative consequence is a difficult circumstance such as a divorce or bankruptcy. Other times, a reproof comes in the form of criticism from our enemies or even our friends.

Although we can't prevent reproofs from coming into our lives, we can choose how we respond to them. In his collection of proverbs, Solomon describes two very different kinds of people who react in two distinct ways to the counsel that failure provides. A wise person learns from reproofs (sometimes referred to as *discipline*) while the foolish person ignores reproofs:

He is on the path of life who heeds instruction,
But he who ignores reproof goes astray.
  (Proverbs 10:17)

Whoever loves discipline loves knowledge,
But he who hates reproof is stupid. (Proverbs 12:1)

Poverty and shame will come to him who neglects
    discipline,
But he who regards reproof will be honored.
  (Proverbs 13:18)

Grievous punishment is for him who forsakes the way;
He who hates reproof will die. (Proverbs 15:10)

A man who hardens his neck after much reproof
Will suddenly be broken beyond remedy. (Proverbs 29:1)

Although Woody Allen paid millions of dollars in legal fees and forfeited box-office receipts for his failure, he admits he learned nothing from those mistakes and would repeat them. Woody Allen is Exhibit A of what Solomon calls "a fool."

How can you keep from falling into the same trap? Instead of continuing to pay for your failure, how can you make your failure start paying you? Here are four vital principles for profiting from your failure rather than messing up for free.

1. Properly Assess Your Failure

Nelson Boswell has said, "The difference between greatness and mediocrity is often how an individual views mistakes."[2]

Remember, failure is not an event but a judgment about an event. Unfortunately, we often make the wrong judgments about our failures, which causes us to wallow in them rather than learn from them. In his book *Learned Optimism,* Martin Seligman describes three distinct perspectives of failure that separate successful people from unsuccessful people.

Permanent or Temporary. "People who give up easily believe the causes of the bad events that happen to them are permanent. The bad events will persist, will always be there to affect their lives," Seligman writes.[3]

This kind of harmful attitude is characterized by words such as *always* or *never.* "I always mess up close friendships" or "I never make good investments."

However, those who recover from failure view it as temporary. "I made a mess of this relationship" or "This stock pick was a bad idea" are examples of responses that refuse to make failure the norm.

Universal or Specific. Some people allow their failure to bleed into every area of their lives. If they're fired from their jobs, they reflexively label every part of their lives as a failure.

79

"They catastrophize," Seligman explains. "When one thread of their life snaps, the whole fabric unravels."[4]

However, those who recover from their mistakes are able to isolate their failure to the appropriate life category.

I know I was pretty hard on Woody Allen earlier, but here's one area in which the famed director excelled. When an interviewer noted with amazement that during the height of his family scandal, Allen still wrote and directed two movies, Allen replied, "Having a stable family life is very nice, but I can work under unstable conditions, too, because—this is not a skill, this is probably a shortcoming—I'm a compartmentalizer."[5]

Frankly, compartmentalizing our failure is a necessary skill if we plan to learn from our mistakes. Failure in one area of our lives doesn't make us a failure in every other area.

Internal or External. Seligman writes, "When bad things happen, we can blame ourselves (internalize), or we can blame other people or circumstances (externalize). People who blame themselves when they fail think they are worthless, talentless, and unlovable.

People who blame external events do not lose self-esteem when bad events strike."[6]

When a woman goes through a divorce, she can conclude "I'm worthless" (internalization) or "This marriage failed because…" (externalization).

I'm not advocating that you blame other people or circumstances for failures that are clearly your fault; as we discussed, you still need to fess up to your mess-ups. However, you can't afford to take responsibility for failures that are clearly out of your control.

2. Learn on Someone Else's Nickel

Sydney Finkelstein understands the educational value of failure. For his best-selling book *Why Smart Executives Fail,* Finkelstein conducted two hundred interviews with intelligent business leaders who had made major mistakes that cost their companies dearly. Rather than focusing on the results of their mistakes, Finkelstein dug deeper to identify the missteps that led to the failures.

For example, at the online grocer Webvan Group Inc., he found that the executives became more interested in fast growth than the quality of service provided, leading to the company's demise. The trendy department store Barney's assumed that consumers in the Midwest would purchase the same style of clothes as customers in New York and ended up closing a number of its outlets. Finklestein's research has resulted in a five-day program at Dartmouth College's Tuck School of Business. While most business courses dissect successful companies, Finklestein believes that "some of the best learning comes from studying the things that go wrong."[7]

Studying things that go wrong can provide invaluable insight into every area of life.

Think about it: wouldn't it be more cost effective if we could learn from the failure fee someone else has already paid rather than paying the tuition ourselves?

Solomon, the wisest man who ever lived, illustrated the importance of learning from other people's mistakes:

I passed by the field of the sluggard

And by the vineyard of the man lacking sense,

And behold, it was completely overgrown with thistles;

Its surface was covered with nettles,

And its stone wall was broken down.

(Proverbs 24:30–31)

As Solomon was taking his morning stroll, he couldn't help but notice the condition of his neighbor's property. The yard was overgrown with weeds, and the fence around the property had fallen down.

Talk about an eyesore!

Had Solomon been like most of us, he would have responded in one of two ways. He might have become angry and said, "I'm going to send a complaint to the homeowners' association. This guy is hurting my property value." Or he might have responded with pride: "I would never allow that to happen to my home."

But instead of becoming angry or prideful over his neighbor's laziness, Solomon chose to learn from it:

When I saw, I reflected upon it;

I looked, and received instruction.

"A little sleep, a little slumber,

A little folding of the hands to rest,"

Then your poverty will come as a robber

And your want like an armed man. (Proverbs 24:32–34)

82   Exactly what did Solomon learn from his neighbor's failure? The Old Testament scholar Derek Kidner summarizes the life lesson Solomon gleaned:

> The wise man will learn while there is time. He knows that
> the sluggard is no freak, but as often as not, an ordinary
> man who has made too many excuses, too many refusals,
> and too many postponements. It has been as imperceptible,
> and as pleasant as falling asleep.[8]

When you see someone fail in his marriage, his business, or his relationship with God, whatever you do, don't gloat over his failure. The Bible warns, "Those who rejoice at the misfortune of others will be punished" (Proverbs 17:5, NLT).

Equally dangerous is to ignore someone else's failure by saying, "That could never happen to me." Again the Bible warns, "If you think you are standing strong, be careful not to fall" (1 Corinthians 10:12, NLT).

Instead, Solomon encourages us to learn from another person's mistakes. Ask yourself these questions when you see someone else fail:

- What wrong assumptions, attitudes, or habits led to his downfall?
- Have I adopted some of those same assumptions, attitudes, or habits in my life?
- What can I do differently to avoid the same pitfall?

3. Instead of Churning over Failure, Start Learning

Failure isn't really failure if you learn from it. However, to profit from our failures we need to take time to carefully analyze our mistakes so we don't repeat them. Analyzing failure correctly requires that we ask the right questions of others, ourselves, and God.

Questions to ask others. Ideally, you have one or two close friends who know you well enough and care about you deeply enough to tell you the truth. Proverbs 12:15 reminds us that "the way of a fool seems right to him, but a wise man listens to advice" (NIV). Here are some questions to ask close friends after you have experienced failure:

- Why do you think I failed?
- What wrong attitudes or assumptions do you think led to my failure?
- If you were I, what would you have done to avoid this mistake?
- Who could provide me wise counsel to help me recover from this failure?

Questions to ask yourself. Consider scheduling a conference with yourself to ask some probing questions, including:

- Have I really failed or just fallen short of an unrealistic goal?

- Is my failure primarily the result of other people, adverse circumstances, or my own wrong choices?
- Whom do I know who has made the same mistake and recovered from it?
- What positive lessons have I already learned from this failure?
- Has my relationship with God been a priority in my life?

Questions to ask God. Remember, no one knows us better or wants to help us more than our heavenly Father. It only makes sense that we should ask Him for assistance in analyzing the cause of our failures. The Bible promises, "But if any of you lacks wisdom, let him ask of God, who gives to all generously and without reproach, and it will be given to him" (James 1:5). Here are some specific questions to ask God after experiencing a great failure:

- Am I doing something in my life that displeases You?
- What changes could I make in my life that would please You the most?
- Am I more concerned with Your approval or the approval of other people?
- Do my standards of success coincide with Your standards of success?

There's no way to overestimate the value of asking the right questions.

Charlie Steinmetz was the engineer who designed the power generators for Henry Ford's automobile plant in Dearborn, Michigan. After Steinmetz retired, the generators quit working, and Ford asked for Steinmetz's help. Steinmetz came into the plant, fiddled with a gauge, pressed a couple of buttons, jiggled a lever, and then after a few hours flipped the switch, and the generators began humming again.

A few days later Henry Ford received a bill from Steinmetz for $10,000. Ford thought the bill was outrageous and responded in a note, "Charlie: It seems awful steep, this $10,000, for a man who for just a little while tinkered around with a few motors." Steinmetz responded with a new, itemized bill and sent it back to Ford. "Henry: For tinkering around with motors, $10; for knowing where to tinker, $9,990."[9]

Knowing the right questions to ask yourself, others, and God can provide invaluable insight for fixing whatever may have gone wrong in your life.

4. Avoid Failure with Your "Advance Warning System"

Pilots of large commercial airliners have on-board warning systems that alert them whenever they are flying too low. A computer-generated voice shouts, "Pull up! Pull up!" when the airplane is in danger of crashing. Heeding the warning system's advice before an accident is much more profitable than sifting through the information provided by voice-data recorders after an accident. If you were a pilot, wouldn't you rather avoid a crash than have someone else learn from your mistake?

Ideally, you have people in your life who will serve as your advance-warning system to help you avoid failure. These are people who know you well, who care about you deeply, and who believe their counsel will be received rather than resented.

Look around you: who will tell you the truth, no matter how much it hurts at the time?

I know a pastor of a large church who announced to his congregation his vision for a multimillion-dollar building project. Leaders in the church were concerned that the project wasn't the best use of resources, but the pastor refused to listen to their counsel and pressed on. Anyone who asked questions about the project was labeled "divisive" and even "demonic" by the pastor and his small circle of friends.

86

The building project caused so much dissension that the pastor resigned the church in the middle of the project, leaving the congregation with a massive debt.

Insulating ourselves from advice by surrounding ourselves with only those who tell us what we want to hear is a guaranteed path to failure.

Consider the experience of King Rehoboam, who followed his father, Solomon, as ruler over Israel. At the beginning of his reign, some of Solomon's advisors approached Rehoboam with a suggestion: "Your father was a great leader, but his building projects have resulted in higher taxes, which are crushing the people." They advised, "If you will lower taxes, the people will follow you forever."

Rehoboam pretended to consider their advice but then called in his handpicked sycophants, who simply reinforced what the king had already planned to do. "If you want to make a name for yourself rather than simply be known as 'Solomon's boy,' you had better initiate more building programs. And that means raising taxes," his cohorts counseled.

Rehoboam followed their suggested course of action, resulting in a civil war that split the kingdom in two.

He should have followed his dad's counsel. Solomon once observed, "Wisdom is found in those who take advice.... The teaching of the wise is a fountain of life, turning a man from the snares of death" (Proverbs 13:10, 14, NIV).

How can you learn from Rehoboam's mistake?

Here's a suggestion worth the price of this book: Go to one or two of your closest friends and say, "I respect your wisdom and know that you care about me. If you ever see me about to make a big mistake in any area of my life—my career, my family, my finances, or my relationship with God—I hope you'll tell me ahead of time."

Then, just as important as soliciting advice, is listening to those friends and receiving with gratitude what they say.

Dale Carnegie is recognized as one of the most successful motivational speakers of all time. His book *How to Win Friends and Influence People* has sold more than fifteen million copies. His Dale Carnegie Institute for Effective Speaking has trained thousands of men and women in the art of effective communication.

But Carnegie wasn't always a success. His early life was marked by consistent failure. Born in poverty, Carnegie determined that he wanted to be a successful speaker. In college he entered a number of speech contests but failed to ever win one. In spite of his hard work in college, he failed to graduate because he could not pass Latin. He moved to New York in hopes of becoming an actor but failed in that career as well.

One day Carnegie applied for a job teaching classes on public speaking at the YMCA. Because he lacked any experience, his employers refused to pay him the usual fee of two dollars per class. Nevertheless, he accepted the job with the condition that he would be paid only if students remained in his class.

Although he'd failed in college and as an actor, Carnegie succeeded in his career at the YMCA. He pored himself into his classes and wrote pamphlets on public speaking that would later become the basis for his megaselling books.

What was the key to Dale Carnegie's successful second act in life?

His biographer writes, "Carnegie rose to fame as one of the most effective trainers of speakers and one of the best-selling authors of all time. Two keys enabled him to turn failure into success: his unwillingness to be stopped by failure, and his willingness to learn from failure."[10]

Simply put, Dale Carnegie refused to mess up for free. And so should you.

But first...

Enjoy Your
Intermission

I n the sports world it's known as halftime—that brief interval
between the first and second half of a game that allows the
players to rest and adjust their strategy while the rest of us restock
our supply of cheese nachos and Diet Coke.

Only the most fickle fan would ever leave a game that early.
Why?

Contests are never won or lost in the first half of the game. No
matter how far ahead or behind a team is in the first half, it is what
happens in the second half that determines the outcome.

I could extend the "life is a game" metaphor ad nauseam.

However, since I have chosen the "life is a performance" theme
for this book, there is another word I want us to consider that is
crucial in recovering from our mistakes: intermission.

Many times the director will schedule a break in a long production to give performers and the audience time to rest and...well, you know. I am probably revealing my age when I recall the days in which long epic movies contained intermissions.

Forty years later I can still tell you when the intermission in *The Sound of Music* occurred. The nun-turned-nanny Maria, confused by her feelings for the captain, decides to leave the family and return to the abbey. Suitcase and guitar in hand, she stands on the steps of the entryway, looks around one last time, and exits. She had failed...or so it seemed.

Fade to black.

Popcorn time!

Had viewers gone home after the first half of the movie, they would have missed the stirring conclusion—where Maria returned to the abbey and experienced her own intermission of sorts. After spending some time on her favorite mountain, she returned to the von Trapps, married the captain, and climbed over the Alps to escape from the Nazis. What a dramatic ending!

In the movie and theatrical world, the intermission is the interval between the first and second half of a production.

In life, intermission is that period of time between our failure and our future.

Our intermission usually begins with some major mistake (or the fallout from that mistake). The curtain seems to come down on our life, and we—as well as others watching—assume that our story is over.

However, our story doesn't have to end with our failure. The curtain can rise again on a wonderful second act. But before that can happen, we need to understand and use this pause between our failure and our future. In case you have not yet grasped the concept of intermission, let me illustrate it for you. Intermission is that period of time between…

- a divorce and the beginning of another meaningful relationship,
- a termination and employment in a job you really desire,
- a bankruptcy and financial solvency,
- a revelation of your immorality and the restoration of your reputation.

While intermissions in movies or plays can be enjoyable, most of us would never choose to endure an intermission in life. This interruption is usually marked by guilt over our failure and apprehension about our future. We wait, and we wonder if the curtain will ever rise again.

God uses this pause to prepare us for an even better second act…if we're willing to cooperate with Him. As you look through the Bible, you'll discover that the Divine Director has always used intermissions in the lives of His people.

For Israel, intermission was the seventy years of Babylonian captivity. God used this time between the people's rebellion and their return to Jerusalem to strengthen their relationship with Him.

For Peter, intermission was the seven weeks between his denial of Christ in Caiaphas's courtyard and his courageous stand for Christ on the Day of Pentecost. It was during this time that the resurrected Lord revealed Himself to Peter and reminded him of his responsibility to "feed my sheep" (John 21:17, NIV).

For Paul, intermission was the three years between his conversion

from the greatest persecutor of the church to the greatest missionary of the church. God used the three years Paul spent in the desert
to teach him the great doctrinal truths he would deliver to the
churches.

Probably the greatest example in Scripture of a God-imposed
intermission is found in the story of Moses. What comes to mind
when you hear the name Moses (besides Charlton Heston)?

The parting of the Red Sea?

The receiving of the Ten Commandments?

The stirring address he gave as the Israelites prepared to enter
the Promised Land?

Do you realize that all these signal events took place in the last
third of Moses's life, after the age of eighty? The first forty years of
Moses's existence are compressed into ten brief verses in Exodus
2:1–10. God miraculously preserved Moses from Pharaoh's slaugh-
ter of the newborn Hebrew males and placed him in Pharaoh's
court:

> After [Moses] had been set outside, Pharaoh's daughter took
> him away and nurtured him as her own son. Moses was
> educated in all the learning of the Egyptians, and he was a
> man of power in words and deeds. (Acts 7:21–22)

Talk about a lucky break! Not only did Moses escape death,
but he ended up in the household of Egypt's most powerful man.
Perhaps Moses would be able to use his relationship with his newly
adopted Grandpa Pharaoh to secure the release of the Israelites. Or
possibly Moses would so dazzle Pharaoh and the Egyptians with

his scholastic ability and powerful oratorical skills that they would gladly acquiesce to his request for Israel's freedom. But God had a different plan. It would be Moses's failure, not his success, that would set the stage for the greatest comeback in Israel's history.

When Moses was about forty years old, he blew it big time. In an instant he made a mistake that would haunt him for decades.

> But when he was approaching the age of forty, it entered his
> mind to visit his brethren, the sons of Israel. And when he
> saw one of them being treated unjustly, he defended him
> and took vengeance for the oppressed by striking down the
> Egyptian. And he supposed that his brethren understood
> that God was granting them deliverance through him, but
> they did not understand.... Moses fled and became an alien
> in the land of Midian. (Acts 7:23–25, 29)

During the first forty years of Moses's life, God had protected him from death and prepared him to be Israel's leader. But in an instant, Moses's temper led him to make a tragic mistake that apparently ruined God's plan for his life. Moses assumed that his murder of the Egyptian soldier had gone unnoticed. But the next day when Moses intervened in a squabble between two Israelites, one of the men asked, "Are you going to kill me just like you killed that Egyptian yesterday?" (See Acts 7:27–28.) Uh-oh!

> When Pharaoh heard of this matter, he tried to kill Moses.
> But Moses fled from the presence of Pharaoh and settled in
> the land of Midian, and he sat down by a well. (Exodus 2:15)

I've often wondered what Moses thought about once he quit running long enough to sit down by the well in the middle of that desert. One mistake had transported him from the palace to the prairie. One moment of uncontrolled rage had sent him from the penthouse to the outhouse! And he would spend a long time there—forty years to be exact. Can you imagine the "if only's" that must have flooded his mind?

If only I had slept in that morning instead of checking out the construction site.

If only I had refused that double shot of espresso in my café latte.

If only I had enrolled in that anger-management class.

Moses was certain that life as he knew it was over. He could forget about being the leader of anything other than a few scraggly sheep in the middle of Nowheresville. The curtain had come down on Moses's dream of leading his people out of bondage into the bountiful land God had promised.

Or so he thought. In reality, Moses was just experiencing an intermission.

> After forty years had passed, an angel appeared to him in the wilderness of Mount Sinai… When Moses saw it, he marveled at the sight; and as he approached to look more closely, there came the voice of the Lord. (Acts 7:30–31)

Do the math for a moment. Moses was forty when he killed the Egyptian. He spent forty years in the desert. That means Moses was eighty years old when God appeared to him and said, *Now it's time for your second act.*

Moses's forty-year desert interlude illustrates three important characteristics about intermissions that we need to understand before we can learn how to profit from the inevitable interruptions in life.

Intermissions are usually imposed, not chosen. After murdering the Egyptian soldier, Moses didn't say to himself, "Whoa! I obviously have some anger issues that need to be resolved before I can be the liberator of Israel. I think I'll take a forty-year sabbatical in the desert."

No, God made that choice for Moses, as He sometimes does for us. From our perspective, intermissions mean waiting...and waiting...and waiting...

Waiting for God to make needed changes in our lives.

Waiting for God to change the hearts of others whom we have hurt.

Waiting for God to work out the circumstances that make our second act possible (in Moses's case, it meant a change of pharaohs).

But waiting times are not wasted times. God's still at work even though we can't always see immediate results. Still, that knowledge doesn't lessen our dislike of intermissions.

Intermissions come at various times in life. In a small town where I once pastored, people used the term *middle-age crazies* to describe the phenomenon pop psychologists have termed *midlife crisis*. This is the time in life, usually between ages thirty-eight and fifty, when people (predominantly, though not exclusively, men) realize that they have more years behind them than in front of them. That realization many times leads to a full-scale panic attack. "I don't want to live the rest of my life like this. I'd better make some changes!" Those changes can include anything from trading in the family sedan for a sports car to trading in a mate for a newer, more energetic (and sometimes synthetic) model.

The sensation that our life clock is ticking more loudly and more quickly can lead us to make some beneficial changes. However, whenever those changes are the result of panic rather careful planning, the result can be disastrous.

Think about Moses. I don't believe it is any coincidence that Moses was approaching forty when he decided to start the revolution without God. Perhaps he was suffering from his own version of the middle-age crazies. *We've been in bondage for four hundred years, and I'm not getting any younger,* Moses concluded. So he led the way in liberating the Israelites.

The only problem was that no Israelites followed him.

Right goal. Wrong time.

Consequently, Moses endured a forty-year intermission, waiting on God's timing.

Although major failures—and the resulting intermissions that follow them—often occur during midlife, they can happen anytime. Divorces, lapses of morality, and financial failures are not confined to one age group. As a pastor, I have seen senior adults mess up just as often as young adults.

Intermissions are of varying lengths. At a football game, the clock on the scoreboard counts down the minutes so fans and players know exactly how much time they have until the second half begins. In the theater the program says, "There will be a twenty-minute intermission" so the audience realizes when they need to return to their seats. And just in case they forget to read the program, the house lights flicker on and off when the second half is about to commence.

But there are no giant clocks, printed programs, or flickering lights in life.

Although a major failure usually signals the beginning of our intermission, we have no idea how long it will be until we begin that new relationship, regain our financial footing, receive a new job offer, or restore a tarnished reputation.

Moses spent forty years in the desert.

Paul spent three years in the desert.

Peter spent six weeks wondering if his failure was final.

Jonah spent three days in the belly of the great fish rethinking his calling.

More important than the length of our intermission is how we use that interlude between our failure and our future. Intermissions can either be a waste of time or an invaluable gift that prepares us for a great second act.

Here's how.

Resist the Urge to Skip Intermissions

We naturally hate the waiting that characterizes intermissions. Part of our dislike for intermissions is the anxiety that accompanies them. We fear the intermission will last indefinitely. If we've gone six months without a job, we worry that we'll always be unemployed. If we've been without a mate for three years, we fear that we'll spend the rest of our lives alone.

Intermissions can also be difficult to endure because of uncomfortable questions from other people. In the sitcom *Everybody Loves Raymond,* the older brother, Robert, is constantly hounded by his intrusive mother because he hasn't remarried after a humiliating divorce.

In one episode the mother cries out, "Why, Robbie? Why can't you find a nice girl and settle down. You're killing me!" Then after a long pause, she looks at him and quietly asks, "Robbie, are you a homosexual?"

The look of disbelief and disgust on his face sends the audience into convulsions of laughter, partly because we can identify with his discomfort in having to endure intrusive questions during an intermission...

"Have you ever considered a career with Amway?"

"Have you ever thought you might be better off single?"

"Didn't you realize what a stupid investment that was?"

"Would you like the name of my cousin's fertility doctor?"

Although the waiting and the uncomfortable questions that accompany intermissions can make us want to rush through them or skip them altogether, doing so can have disastrous consequences. For example, have you ever wondered why the divorce statistics for second marriages are higher than for first marriages?

Simple answer: not understanding the value of intermissions.

My father was married to my mother for thirty-five years before she died of cancer at age fifty-five. He was so overcome with grief and terrified by the prospect of being alone the rest of his life that he rushed through his intermission, entered into a disastrous second marriage, and died shortly afterward. My father was an extremely intelligent man. *How could he have made such a poor choice of a mate?* many of us wondered.

My dad was like many people who try to avoid their intermissions by rushing into a new relationship, a new job, or a new financial scheme. They become victims of the blizzard effect, a concept my friend Bobb Biehl explained to me many years ago.

A blizzard is the result of small pieces of snow being driven by wind, causing blurred vision. These tiny pieces of frozen precipitation are inconsequential by themselves. But in a storm they can paralyze your ability to move. The only way to stop a blizzard is to turn down the wind.

99

Storms blow into our lives, and suddenly the smallest details of our lives are swirling around in front of us and distorting our perspective. This is absolutely the worst time to make a major decision! Before we can see clearly, we must allow the wind to subside.

Sometimes we can turn off the wind ourselves. Have you ever felt as if circumstances were moving so quickly that you couldn't see clearly enough to make the simplest decision, such as what to do next? Spending a half day or even a half hour in a quiet place away from other people, the telephone, and e-mail is a simple way to turn down the wind.

However, major storms that are caused by our failures cannot be turned off so easily or quickly. We just have to wait for the wind to die down and resist the urge to move forward when our vision is impaired. But remember, waiting time does not have to be wasted time. There are several important things we can do while we are waiting out the storm.

Refresh Your Physical and Emotional Batteries

My friend Howard Hendricks said, "Sometimes the most spiritual thing you can do is take a nap!" The Old Testament prophet Elijah discovered that truth after he failed to exercise faith and gave in to fear. Elijah had just taken a bold stand for God on Mount Carmel and successfully demonstrated to Israel that Jehovah, not Baal, was the true God.

Queen Jezebel, the chief promoter of Baal worship in Israel, wasn't exactly thrilled when she heard that Elijah had not only humiliated her god but had also decimated more than four hundred of her false prophets. When she threatened his life, instead of taking a stand, the prophet ran...and ran...and ran until he collapsed under a juniper tree and asked God to take his life.

Instead, God encouraged him to take a nap.

When Elijah awakened, he found a jar of water and a cake delivered by an angel (this may be where we get angel food cake!). After eating and drinking, Elijah went back to sleep. He kept repeating the process of eating and sleeping until his perspective was restored and he was ready to return to business.

Failure can exact a devastating emotional and physical toll on our lives. God understands that reality and graciously provides us with intermissions during which we can refresh ourselves for our second act. Instead of refusing the gift, use the gift!

For example, if you are facing termination from your job, negotiate with your employer for as many weeks or months of severance pay as possible. Don't allow pride to keep you from asking for more. After all, at this point you have nothing to lose!

If you receive three months of severance pay, you obviously

need to use most of that time to secure a new position. But use the first week or two for something you've always wanted to do and have never had time for: a trip, a project around the house, a short-term class in a subject that has always fascinated you. Far from being a waste of time, these diversions will reenergize you as you prepare for your next act.

Reflect on Where You've Been and Where You Want to Go

One of the upsides to failure is that it provides us with both the motivation and opportunity to stop what we are doing and make midcourse corrections in our lives.

Some of our intermission time should be used for personal refreshment. But we should also use a portion to reflect on what we have learned from our failure (see the previous chapter for key questions to help you) and to answer some directional questions that will help us prepare for our second act.

By the way, you don't have to be unemployed to experience a profitable intermission. Use a day off or several days of vacation to find a place where you can turn down the wind and ask yourself directional questions such as...

- What three things would I like to accomplish before I die?
- Am I in the job I want to be doing ten years from now?
- What do I feel passionate about in life?
- What do other people think I'm gifted to do?
- What would an ideal day be for me? (Where would I be living, what job would I have, what people would be around me?)

- Who is the one person who knows me best and loves me most and with whom I could have a heart-to-heart talk about my situation?

Renew Your Relationship with God

I hate silence. My mother-in-law is taking my wife and two daughters on a girls-only trip in a few weeks, and I'm absolutely dreading four days of coming home to an empty house. I'm already planning where I can go and what I can do to avoid the aloneness. I easily identify with the philosopher Blaise Pascal's words about our natural aversion to silence:

> I have discovered that all the unhappiness of men arises from one single fact, that they cannot stay quietly in their own chamber. We do not seek that easy and peaceful lot which permits us to think of our unhappy conditions, nor the dangers of war, nor the labour of office, but the bustle which averts these thoughts of ours, and amuses us. Reasons why we like the chase better than the quarry. Hence it comes that men so much love noise and stir; hence it comes that the prison is so horrible a punishment; hence it comes that the pleasure of solitude is a thing incomprehensible.[1]

Although most of us have an addiction to activity, we desperately need times of solitude, especially after experiencing a major failure in life. Solitude and silence not only provide an opportunity to reflect on the past and visualize the future, but they allow us to hear from the One whom we most need—especially in a crisis.

I believe that God is continually speaking to us; we just don't always hear His voice above the clamor of our busyness. That was Elijah's problem. Although he was a successful prophet who worked tirelessly for God, he lost his personal connection with God and began to feel as if he were all alone. His sense of isolation led to desperation as he fled from Jezebel and ended up under a tree ready to trade in his prophet's mantle.

After some much-needed R and R, Elijah traveled to Mount Horeb and took up residence in a cave. God told Elijah to step outside the cave. There the prophet witnessed a spectacular display of God's power, complete with an earthquake, wind, and fire. But then the Bible makes an interesting observation:

> But the LORD was not in the wind.... The LORD was not in
> the earthquake.... The LORD was not in the fire; and after
> the fire a sound of a gentle blowing. When Elijah heard it,
> he wrapped his face in his mantle and went out and stood
> in the entrance of the cave. And behold, a voice came to
> him. (1 Kings 19:11–13)

God spoke through the silence rather than through the noise. It was while Elijah was inside the cave, rather than on the mountain, that he heard a small, gentle voice reminding him of his calling and giving him the direction he needed for his second act.

If you're experiencing an intermission in your life right now, don't despise it. Recognize it as a perfect time for you to listen to God's still, small voice.

How?

If you are unaccustomed to spending time alone with God, don't overdo it by trying to spend an entire week or even an entire day by yourself.

Instead, find a secluded spot where you can spend two or three uninterrupted hours.

First, I suggest that you allow God to speak to you through His Word. When you read Scripture, you can know that you are listening to nothing other than the voice of God. Consider reading Psalm 34, which extols the faithfulness of God, or Psalm 51, which describes the forgiveness of God. Romans 8 (my favorite chapter in the Bible) reminds us of the love of God, from which we can never be separated.

Next, I recommend you take a good Christian book with you that emphasizes the character of God, such as A. W. Tozer's *The Knowledge of the Holy,* J. Oswald Sanders's *The Pursuit of the Holy,* or J. I. Packer's *Knowing God.* Read a chapter or two in one of these classics. Remember, you're trying to reconnect with a Person, not a set of ideas. Reading what these godly men have discovered about God will encourage you.

Finally, allow God to speak to your particular situation by asking Him the questions I suggested in the previous chapter:

- What am I doing in my life that displeases You?
- What do You want me to do that I'm not now doing?
- Am I more interested in pleasing You or pleasing others?
- Am I defining success and failure by Your standards or other people's standards?

Remember, the Curtain Will Rise Again!

Failure seems so final. And the intermissions that usually follow only confirm our deepest fear that life as we know it is over. We can easily forget that intermissions are simply commas, not periods, in our life story.

Consider the experience of Jesus Christ. From a human perspective, the Lord had failed. What started as a growing movement embraced by thousands was reduced to a handful of followers who denied they even knew Him when the going got tough. By all appearances, His dream for a new kingdom had failed. He died alone, deserted by His friends and alienated from His heavenly Father.

But the story wasn't over.

And then they put his body in a cave. That was their big mistake. His body was there for three days. But they could not keep him there. They forgot that God does some of his best work in caves. The cave is where God resurrects dead things.[2]

At some point in your life you will find yourself in a cave. You'll be tempted to think that the death of a relationship, career, dream, or reputation means that your life is over. But it isn't. The pause in your life story isn't permanent. It's simply a prelude to what can be a spectacular second act.

Begin Your Second Act Now

Tempus fugit. Time flies…except when you're sitting through a graduation ceremony, standing in the wrong line at the bank, or enduring an intermission in your life story. That interval between your past failure and your future success can seem endless. But as we saw in the previous chapter, waiting time is not wasted time. Intermissions are opportunities for refreshment, reflection, and sometimes redirection.

In a performance, however, everyone knows when the second act is about to begin: the lights go down, sometimes the orchestra begins an overture, and the curtain rises indicating that intermission is now over.

If only life were that simple. Wouldn't you love for God to give you an unmistakable signal when your second act was about to begin? Waiting would be a lot easier if you knew when you'd find a new job, enter a new relationship, see your balance sheet turn from red to black, or stop paying for a lapse of judgment.

Nevertheless, intermissions are not interminable. Intermissions do eventually end, signaling that the curtain is about to rise again. In this chapter we are going to discover five important principles for discerning when our intermission is over and how we can pre-

pare for a successful second act in life.

SAY GOOD-BYE TO REGRETS

That exhortation is more than the title of one of my books (pardon the plug); it is a crucial principle for a new beginning. You can never start your second act if you are still reliving the failures of your first act. Remember the movie *Groundhog Day* with Bill Murray? Every morning Murray would awaken to the radio playing "I've Got You, Babe" and find himself reliving the same day. In the movie, it was hilarious. In life, reliving your experiences can be tragic.

Author Erwin McManus describes the paralyzing effect:

One moment in the past continues to haunt every moment of your life. A moment in your history that steals from you all the moments in the future. Is there a moment you keep reliving again and again? To relive the past is to relinquish the future. If you are willing to let go of the past, then you are ready to step into the future. When you choose to re-main stuck in a moment you become incapable of seizing your divine moments.[1]

Perhaps the writer of Hebrews had this truth in mind when he encouraged us to...

Lay aside every encumbrance and the sin which so easily entangles us, and let us run with endurance the race that is set before us. (Hebrews 12:1)

A runner can never expect to win a race while looking back at ground he has already covered. He can't simultaneously relive a past stumble and concentrate on the future challenge. He's either focused on what's behind him or what's in front of him.

I realize that letting go of regrets is easier said than done. If you find it difficult to focus on future possibilities rather than on past failures, three realities can help you release your regrets over your mistakes.

First is **the impossibility of undoing your mistake.** Only in movies do people get the chance to travel back in time and make different choices. However, every day we can choose to engage in mental time travel and relive the pain of past mistakes. That's a trip you can't afford to take.

Next is **the reality of God's forgiveness.** When you accept God's offer of forgiveness, He takes your failures, nails them to the cross of Jesus Christ, and declares them paid in full. There's nothing you can add to the payment He has already made for you. Since God remembers our iniquities no more and casts our sins into the depths of the sea, why should we insist on dredging them back up?

Third is **the possibility of future change.** You've probably heard of the Nobel Prize, which awards excellence in the fields of literature, physics, peace, and economics. But you may not be aware of the history of those awards.

Alfred Nobel was a Swedish chemist who made his fortune by inventing explosives and licensing their manufacture to foreign governments for the production of weapons. When Nobel's brother died, the newspaper accidentally ran Alfred's obituary instead of his brother's. Alfred Nobel had the unique opportunity to read how others would remember him: the man who invented dynamite and enabled countries to more effectively destroy one another.

Regretting that he'd only be remembered as a merchant of death, Nobel decided to rechannel the remainder of his life to more productive efforts. Using a sizable amount of his net worth, he established the Nobel Prizes to encourage achievements that would benefit humanity. Today few people know that Alfred Nobel invented dynamite. Instead, they remember him as someone who had a positive influence on the world.[2]

Although we can't remake past choices or regain lost time and opportunities, we can reshape our tomorrows as well as our eternity. That's what second acts are all about.

PAY ATTENTION TO SEASONAL CHANGES

One practical benefit of letting go of regrets over the past is that it frees you to be more attuned to the present. People who constantly relive their mistakes are oblivious to changes around them that may signal the beginning of their second act.

Remember the movie *Mary Poppins?*

Near the beginning of the film, a weather vane makes a 180-degree turn, and the chimney sweep, Bert, recognizes that something is in the air. That something is the arrival of the magical, musical nanny Mary Poppins. By the end of the movie, when the weather vane turns again, it's time for Mary Poppins to leave (until the Disney folks decide to bring her back in a rerelease or DVD).

All-knowing weather vanes would make life a lot easier. If only we knew ahead of time when a major change was coming, we could prepare for it. Obviously, no instrument exists that can predict life changes. But that doesn't mean we are simply reduced to going with the flow.

God wants you to be able to discern changes in your circumstances that portend a major turning point in your life so you can be prepared to take advantage of that change. The Bible continually extols the value of wisdom, the skill to live according to God's plan. One by-product of wisdom is the ability to discern major turning points in our lives.

For example, in the Old Testament, the sons of Issachar are described as "men who understood the times, with knowledge of what Israel should do" (1 Chronicles 12:32). Just as a savvy politician knows when the conditions are right to enter a race and challenge an incumbent, these men were able to discern that conditions were optimal for a major political upheaval in Israel. Sensing that the time was ripe for David to expand his kingdom to include all of Israel, these men decided to cast their lot with him. Their hunch turned out to be correct.

What does all this have to do with second acts in life? We need to be able to discern when our intermission is over and it's time to begin our second act. Prolonging an intermission can be as destructive as skipping an intermission.

How can you know when it's time to begin your second act? Look for changes in…

Your attitude. Have you quit blaming others for your failure and accepted responsibility for your mistakes? Can you articulate the lessons you have learned from your failure?

Your emotions. Do you still feel emotionally and physically drained from the aftermath of your failure, or are you starting to feel refreshed from your intermission? When other people refer to your mistakes, are you defensive, or can you discuss them objectively?

Your circumstances. A job offer that comes out of nowhere, a dinner invitation from someone you are interested in, or a child's leaving home may signal that you are about to enter a new era in your life. Even a seemingly negative circumstance can actually be the prelude to a positive second act, as it was for the Old Testament character Jacob.

You may recall that Jacob had worked for his uncle Laban for twenty years. Although their relationship had been volatile, Jacob eventually became content with his life and imagined he would spend the remainder of his days tending sheep, far removed from the Promised Land of Canaan, where he had once lived.

But God had a different plan. Act 2 of Jacob's story involved returning to the Promised Land, reconciling with his estranged brother, Esau, and renewing his commitment to God. How did Jacob discern it was time to leave Laban and return home?

Jacob saw the attitude of Laban, and behold, it was not
friendly toward him as formerly. (Genesis 31:2)

Instead of becoming bitter over his uncle's unexpected and
sudden hostility toward him, Jacob discerned that God was using
that change in attitude to move him and his family back to their
home so they could experience a new beginning.

Can you sense that an important weather vane is turning?

Are winds of change blowing in your life right now?

If so, it may be time for your second act to commence.

DEVELOP YOUR SECOND-ACT SCRIPT

While living in Dallas, I had the opportunity to know the late
Mary Crowley, the founder of the Home Interiors Company, which
has grossed hundreds of millions of dollars through the years. Mary
started the company during her second act in life. A recently
divorced mother with two small children, she was desperate to provide for her family. After letting go of the regrets of a marital failure and sensing that her negative circumstances could actually be a
motivation for a change in her life, Mary developed a plan to start
a direct-sales business that would not only take care of her financial needs but would be in keeping with her life purpose to glorify
God. Her remarkable leadership skills also positioned her to be the
first woman to serve on the board of the Billy Graham Evangelis-
tic Association.

Many of the largest Christian organizations in the world have been the beneficiaries of her phenomenal financial success. Mary understood that successful second acts don't just happen but are the result of careful planning.

Benjamin Franklin once observed, "I have always thought that one Man of tolerable Abilities may work great Changes, and accomplish great Affairs among Mankind, if he first forms a good Plan, and, cutting off all Amusements or other Employments that would divert his Attention, makes the Execution of that same plan his sole Study and Business."[3]

No wonder Franklin's second act was filled with such phenomenal accomplishments as the invention of bifocal glasses (at age seventy-eight), negotiating peace with Britain after the Revolutionary War (at age seventy-seven), and the writing of the Constitution (at age eighty-one).

Franklin understood the importance of formulating a plan and working that plan.

I frequently encounter people—especially Christians—who are skeptical of planning.

"Who knows the future?" or "Shouldn't we just trust God?" are some common objections to writing out a detailed plan to overcome a failure.

Yet the Bible continually emphasizes the value of planning:

Commit your works to the LORD,
And your plans will be established. (Proverbs 16:3)

Prepare plans by consultation,
And make war by wise guidance. (Proverbs 20:18)

The plans of the diligent lead surely to advantage,
But everyone who is hasty comes surely to poverty.
(Proverbs 21:5)

Obviously, any plans we make can be overridden by God. He
always has the final say in every aspect of our lives.

However, the reality of God's sovereignty does not negate the
value of planning for our second act.

I suggest you get a legal tablet or a spiral notebook and spend
half a day writing out your second-act script. The plan or script
you develop should include four essential components:

- **Clarification of the problem:** In a word or a phrase,
  write down the failure from which you are trying to
  recover, such as divorce, financial insolvency, wrong career
  choice, or termination. For this exercise, let's assume you
  have experienced a financial disaster that has left you
  with insufficient funds to meet your current and future
  needs.

- **Visualization of the goal:** In a sentence, describe your
  desired outcome for this problem. For example, "I would
  like to have enough money so I don't have to constantly
  worry about finances" is both a worthy and a biblical goal.
  The writer of Proverbs prayed, "Give me neither poverty
  nor riches; feed me with the food that is my portion"
  (Proverbs 30:8). He understood that having too little
  money might cause him to steal and having too much
  might cause him to forget his need for God. How would
  you summarize your ideal financial situation?

- **Identification of the obstacles.** What barriers are keeping you from your intended goal? List the obstacles that must be overcome before you can experience your desired outcome during your second act. For example, if your problem is financial, your list of obstacles might include:

    Maxed-out credit cards

    Insufficient monthly income

    No savings for children's college or my retirement

- **Specification of Action Steps.** Once you have identified the obstacles to your goal, write down specific action steps you can take to remove those obstacles. For example, under "insufficient monthly income" you might specify several ways to improve your cash flow each month, including reducing your expenses, finding a higher paying job, or securing a second job. Each of those ideas may generate additional steps, such as turning down the thermostat, switching to a cheaper long-distance carrier, checking on different job possibilities with friends in your industry, or developing a plan to ask your employer for a raise.

Ideally, your second-act script will contain a number of specific action steps you can take right now to ensure a successful new beginning.

LEARN TO TRAVEL IN A FOG

We used to live in an area near a lake where early-morning fog was a way of life. Understanding the dangers of driving on a busy highway with limited visibility, I thought it would be more prudent to wait until the fog lifted before I headed for work. However, I soon realized I couldn't afford to lose several hours a day waiting for 100 percent visibility. I needed to learn how to travel in the fog.

It would be nice if we could see our future with perfect clarity. We could plan more intelligently. We could move forward in our plans with greater speed and confidence. Collisions with adverse circumstances and people would be rare.

Obviously, no one can know the future except God. Nevertheless, some people refuse to act until the fog lifts and they have a perfect view of what lies ahead. So they wait…and wait…and wait.

If we are going to experience a great second act, we must learn to travel in the fog. Moving forward with limited visibility requires…

Need. To be honest, the only reason I didn't wait at home until the fog cleared is because my employer wouldn't let me. Eventually I had to start moving or risk losing my job. A mild case of desperation motivated me to action. Before you will risk moving forward in the fog of the unknown, you will need to feel a holy discontent. Only when you can no longer stand your present situation will you be sufficiently motivated to take that first step into the unknown.

Remember the cartoon character Popeye? In every episode there came a turning point when Popeye was so frustrated over his situation (usually losing his lovely girlfriend, Olive Oyl, to his muscular antagonist, Brutus) that he said, "That's all I can stands. I can't stands no more!" After gulping down a can of spinach, his biceps began to bulge, and Popeye was ready for action.

Beth, a recently divorced mother of three, had not worked outside the home in twenty years. When a friend offered to recommend her for a job, she hesitated to accept the offer. She barely knew how to turn on a computer and doubted she possessed the stamina to work forty hours a week and still care for her children.

But Beth was tired of having to refuse her children's every request for clothes, makeup, or special treats. She hated staying home by herself every day and reliving the mistakes of her twenty-year marriage. Only because she couldn't stand her situation any longer did she take the job. When I recently asked Beth how she was doing, she replied, "I'm making it—barely. But I'm happier than I've been in a year."

What is it in your life that you "can't stands no more"? Working at that dead-end job? Living alone? Worrying about your finances? You will never be willing to travel in the fog of uncertainty until you feel a desperate need to move beyond your present circumstances.

Movement. Once you have your Popeye moment and are motivated to launch your second act, you are ready to move forward. If your visibility is limited, you can move slowly and cautiously, just as you would while driving in a fog. The important thing is to start moving.

One writer observes that the apostles and the early church did not always do everything correctly. They made mistakes.

They didn't get everything right. The early communities were far from perfect. No one, not even the apostles, had a perfect understanding. Many of us want a map, but what we get is a compass. We are not given a detailed outline of how we should live each day. We are given a due north, a direction we should move toward. On this journey one thing becomes certain: when you move forward on what you know, things become clearer. When you refuse to act, what you do not know paralyzes you.[4]

Let me encourage you to select one simple action step from your second-act script and just do it. Make that phone call, write that letter, or schedule that appointment. You will be surprised how much easier it will then be for you to take the next step and then the step after that one.

Faith. Fortunately, we have a God who can see through the fog. Once we sense He is leading us to begin our second act, we can take that first step with the assurance of His protection as we keep moving forward.

When Moses and the Israelites saw the weather vane of Pharaoh's attitude do a 180, they knew it is was time to throw their tunics in a suitcase, strap on their sandals, and start marching toward the Promised Land. But a giant obstacle stood between them and their desired future: the Red Sea. With the Egyptians in hot pursuit behind them, and this massive body of water in front of them, they had a choice: be slaughtered by the Egyptians or drown. What a choice!

While the Israelites lamented and complained about their dilemma, God commanded them to do something that made absolutely no sense:

Tell the sons of Israel to go forward. (Exodus 14:15)

Go forward? Was God directionally challenged? Couldn't He see that giant body of water in front of them that He had created?

You know the rest of the story. God miraculously parted the waters so the Israelites could pass through the Red Sea. Only when Israel made it to the other side, did God close the sea and destroy the Egyptians who pursued them.

There is an unnamed hero in this story who gets little recognition (not Moses—he got a movie made about him!). It's the guy at the head of the line who had to take that first step while Moses stood on the side, stretching out his hands over the sea. He never gets much attention, but he should.

Can you imagine the faith required to take that first step onto the land that only hours earlier had formed the bottom of the sea? Looking at the massive walls of water on his right and left, I'm sure he was tempted to think, *Maybe I should pray about this a little longer. Perhaps I should ask God for another sign, just to be on the safe side.* But God had said, "Go forward."

Yes, the water could come crashing down at any moment. No, the future was not all that clear. But that first Israelite had already experienced his Popeye moment. He was tired of life in Egypt and believed that the same God who was leading him to take the first step would protect him until he reached the other side.

Appreciate the Importance of NOW

Television interviewer Barbara Walters was once asked about the greatest lesson she had ever learned. "In life there are no dress rehearsals," she replied.

No dress rehearsals and no repeat performances. Once the Divine Director gives us the cue, the time to begin our second act is now.

David Jeremiah writes about a scholar who once surveyed the Bible to discover the most significant words in Scripture, such as the saddest word in the Bible, the happiest word in the Bible, and so on. The most dangerous word in the Bible?

Tomorrow.

He concluded that the word *tomorrow* is a thief that robs dreamers of their dreams and the gifted of great accomplishments. The great pastor Charles Spurgeon concurred, writing, "Tomorrow, tomorrow, tomorrow! Alas, tomorrow never comes! It is in no calendar except the almanac of fools."[5]

I've always thought it ironic that we humans, whom the Bible describe as vapors that appear for a little while and then vanish, squander time. Yet the eternal God, who exists from everlasting to everlasting, values time. To us, time is limitless. To God, time is priceless. Our opportune time to begin is tomorrow. God's favorite time is today:

This is the day which the LORD has made. (Psalm 118:24)

But encourage one another…as long as it is still called "Today." (Hebrews 3:13)

Today if you hear His voice… (Hebrews 3:7)

Has some significant weather vane in your life turned? Have you sensed God's signaling you that it's time to begin your second act? If so, stop waiting until…

your kids are grown,

your mortgage is gone,

your future is certain,

your hurts have healed.

God has given you no guarantee of a tomorrow (not here on earth anyway). And the past is gone forever. All you have is today.

A sign on a businessman's desk asks, "In twenty years what will you wish you had done today?" Somehow I believe you already know how you would answer that question. Why have any regrets twenty years from now? Why delay taking that first step that is so clear? "Today if you hear His voice..."

The lights are dimming; the orchestra is tuning; the Director is giving you the cue. The time to begin your second act is *now*.

PREPARE FOR THE GRAND FINALE

O nce upon a time there was a poor, old man who owned a beautiful white horse that was the envy of everyone in the small village where he lived. One day the old man discovered that the horse was missing from the stable. The townspeople said to him, "You're a stupid old man. We told you someone would steal your horse. You have been cursed."

The old man replied, "Don't go so far as to say that. Simply say that the horse is not in the stable. That's all you can say; the rest is a judgment."

The people protested. "You make us out to be fools," one representative cried. "It's obvious to everyone that your horse has been stolen and that you are cursed."

After two weeks the horse returned. He had run away, and now he came back with a dozen wild horses. The villagers gathered in front of the old man's house and said, "Forgive us. We were wrong. Obviously you are not cursed. You are blessed because you have thirteen beautiful white horses."

The old man replied, "Once again you have made a judgment you are not prepared to make. All you can say is that the horse returned with twelve others. Whether this is a blessing or a curse, only God knows."

The old man had an only son who worked at taming the wild horses. One day he fell from one of the horses and broke both his legs. The townspeople once again offered their insight. "You were right, and we were wrong," their representative said. "We thought the horses were a blessing, but we judged too quickly. Obviously they were a curse since your only son has broken both his legs, and now there is no one to help you in your old age."

The old man couldn't believe what he was hearing. "Why are you so intent on judging? All you can say with certainty is that my son broke both his legs. Who knows whether it's a blessing or a curse."

A few weeks later, war broke out in the adjacent country. All the young men were drafted into service. But the old man's son was exempted because of his injury. The people in the village once again came to visit the old man. "You were right, and we were wrong. Our sons are going into battle to be slaughtered. But your son's accident turned out to be a blessing."

The old man sighed. "When will you ever learn? All you can say with certainty is that your sons went to battle and my son stayed home. Whether it's a blessing or curse, only God knows."

Our culture celebrates the ability to make snap judgments.

Commentators offer instant analysis of a presidential address. Television news networks seem more interested in being first than being right when covering major disasters. Best-selling business books like *Blink* explain how to size up any situation in a few minutes.

However, our propensity for quick judgments can lead us to the wrong conclusion, especially when it comes to our mistakes. To allow one lapse of judgment, one wrong choice, or one missed opportunity to define our entire lives is to be as shortsighted as the townspeople in the previous parable.

Throughout this book we have been comparing life to a performance during which we step onto the world stage and play our assigned parts for the seventy to eighty years we may have. Even though at times we may miss a cue or blow a line, that doesn't stop our performance. As the old saying goes, "It ain't over until the fat lady sings." As long as you are still breathing, you have time to recover from your failure.

The apostle Paul, describing the difficulties he and the other apostles endured, wrote:

We have become a spectacle to the world, both to angels and to men. (1 Corinthians 4:9b)

The word translated "spectacle" is *theatron,* from which we derive our word *theater.* Eugene Peterson's paraphrase of the first half of this verse in The Message captures Paul's thoughts perfectly:

God has put us who bear his Message on stage in a theater in which no one wants to buy a ticket.

Your life—especially the difficult parts—will never make sense until you see it as part of a larger, eternal drama being played out on the world's stage for both a visible and invisible audience. This epic drama began a long time ago—when Lucifer chose to rebel against his Creator—and will answer several vital questions:

Who will ultimately prevail in the eternal battle between the kingdom of God and the kingdom of Satan?

126

Who is the more worthy ruler of the universe?

Will Satan be able to turn God's creatures—like you and me—against our Creator?

The visible audience for this drama is those around you who are carefully watching how you respond to the joys and disappointments, the blessings and adversity, the successes and failures that come your way. But as we play our assigned role in this universal drama for the life span God gives us, there is also a vast unseen audience watching our performance, including God, the angels in heaven, the demons on earth (and some confined under the earth), and Satan.

You'll never be able to properly evaluate the whole of your life—including your failures—until you understand the duration of this drama, your role in it, and your reward.

THE DURATION: IT'S LONGER
THAN YOU SUPPOSE

My biggest financial blowup occurred a number of years ago (hopefully). Apparently I was on some organization's sucker list and received a four-color brochure promising me unimaginable riches by investing a small amount in silver futures. By investing just a few thousand dollars, I could control tens of thousands of dollars in silver contracts, I was promised.

I took the bait.

For the first few days, I was checking silver prices hourly and saw them rise, along with the value of my investment. What I didn't realize—or chose to ignore—was that commodity prices can go down as well as up, and when you're highly leveraged as I was, your losses multiply exponentially.

The guy at the investment firm, who'd been so friendly when I was considering investing with him, now starting phoning me on a regular basis with margin calls.

In case you're not a sophisticated investor like yours truly, a margin call is basically a demand to send a large chunk of money immediately to cover your ever-increasing losses or risk having your kneecaps come in contact with an unwelcome baseball bat. I barely met my margin call, got out of the silver business, and spent months trying to recover from my losses.

Financial planners often use the term *time horizon* when advising clients. Before a good planner will offer advice about the right mix of stocks, bonds, and cash (but hopefully no silver futures) in an investment portfolio, he'll want to know the client's investment time horizon: how long do you have before you'll need the money you're investing?

If retirement is twenty years away, you can afford to take some risks, since you have time to recover from any mistakes.

However, if you will need the money in three years, you need to avoid risk since you don't have time to recover from any misjudgment.

Had my investment fiasco occurred when I was sixty rather than thirty, I would have been in trouble. But fortunately, as much as my loss hurt at the time, today it's little more than a funny story and a learned lesson about avoiding get-rich-quick schemes.

Knowing your time horizon not only helps you make financial decisions, but it can help you place your other failures in proper perspective. If you make a major mistake in your twenties with your money, career, or relationships, you're more likely to have decades to recover from that mistake. However, if that mistake occurs in your sixties, the results can be catastrophic...or so it seems.

But I have waited until this final chapter to relate to you the single most liberating truth I've ever learned about recovering from failures in life. Before I share it, I want to tell you how I discovered it.

In chapter 5, I described hiring a consultant when I was forty to help me map out the remainder of my ministry. The first thing he did was ask me to draw a time line representing my life and mark on that line when I anticipated retiring and where I was now. The line looked like this:

0_____40_____65—Retirement

"Why did you end at age sixty-five?" he asked. "Is there a policy in your church that requires you to retire at sixty-five?"

"No," I told him, "I assumed that since most people retired

then, I would as well. Besides, both my parents died of cancer before age sixty-five, and I assumed I would have a short life."

"How do you feel about having only twenty-five years of ministry left?" he probed.

"Honestly, it frightens me," I confessed. "I have so many things I still want to do, but I don't feel like I have enough time."

The consultant then took his pen and extended the line to age eighty. "What if you lengthened your time line by fifteen years? Would you feel better about your life and plans for the future?"

Of course I would! "But how is that possible?" I asked.

"You're assuming that because your parents died early, you will too. But from what you've told me, you're doing a lot of things to protect your health that your parents never did. You exercise, eat right, and visit the doctor regularly. There's no reason to think you won't have a longer life."

Extending my time horizon instantly relieved me of the regrets I had over some poor choices during the first forty years of my life; it also reenergized me as I thought about my future potential.

Obviously, no consultant can prolong your life. God is the One who determines the number of years we have here on earth.

But here's the liberating truth I want to share with you: you are going to live forever. If you're a Christian, God has given you eternal life, and that means your time horizon is forever. Bruce Wilkinson uses the illustration of the dot and the line to illustrate the impact of that truth. Place a dot on a piece of paper, and then draw a line from that dot all the way across that piece of paper, like this:

The dot represents the seventy or eighty years you have on earth, but the line represents your life after you die. Tragically, most people expend all of their energy living for the dot and give very little attention to preparing for the never-ending line.

Now let me apply that reality to recovering from failure. Assume that, like Moses, you experience a major failure around the age of forty. Although up to that time you'd experienced some successes, that major failure is the defining event of your life. Your one mistake has seemingly negated all the good things in your life to that point.

However, after a brief intermission, you're ready to begin your second act at age forty-one. Nevertheless, you can't help but wonder, *Do I have enough time to recover from such a colossal mistake?*

When you understand that your time frame is not limited to your few years here on earth, it changes your perspective about your failure. God has given you an eternal time horizon. Your second act goes on and on and on and on, making your first act only a prelude to the real show.

YOUR ROLE: IT'S DIFFERENT THAN YOU THINK

Kenneth Ulmer relates a story about a criminology course he took in college. He says that he "cut that class every which way but loose." But when he heard about an assignment to write a research paper, he poured himself into the project, hoping he could compensate for his frequent absences.

The professor returned Ulmer's paper with this evaluation: "Good paper, great content, great research." But on the paper was

130

a giant F circled in red, accompanied by an explanation: "But this was not the assignment." Ulmer says that he learned a valuable lesson that day: "It does not matter how well you do what you do, if you do not do what you should do."[1]

What a great principle to remember for completing any assignment, especially the one God has given to each of us. If we don't understand the role God assigned us to perform in this life, how can we accurately evaluate our successes or failures?

The executive who finally receives the title of chairman, the worker who accumulates a million dollars in his 401(k) plan, and the pastor who builds a church of ten thousand may consider themselves successful...until the day they hear God say, "But that wasn't the assignment."

Similarly, some people who stumble in life through a broken marriage, bankruptcy, termination, or unrealized dreams still have the possibility of hearing God say, "Well done, good and faithful servant!"

How is that possible? When we connect our mistakes to the role God has assigned us, then what we term *failure* can actually become a success.

So what part has God assigned to us for the years we are on earth's stage? What's our role? Simple. It's the same role that Jesus had during His thirty-three years here on earth:

I glorified You [God the Father] on the earth, having accomplished the work which You have given Me to do. (John 17:4)

Our role is to glorify God during the time we are on life's stage. The word *glorify* is one of those overused religious terms that few people really understand. To "glorify God" simply means to make God look good to other people. Glorifying God involves turning the spotlight away from us and shining it on the Divine Director of the eternal drama in which we each play a minor role. That's what Jesus did while here on earth. Jesus's words in John 17:4 could be paraphrased this way:

> God, I played the part You assigned Me to play. I made You look good while I was here on earth.

What does all this have to do with our failures? Our mistakes provide some of the best opportunities for us to make God look good. A spotlight can shine in only one direction at a time. When we're successful, the spotlight is directed toward us ("Isn't she talented!" "Isn't he shrewd!" "Aren't they a model couple!"). But when we fail, our mistake gives us the opportunity to turn the spotlight away from us and onto God, who is willing to forgive and restore. That reality led to Paul's observation:

> "Power is perfected in weakness." Most gladly, therefore, I
> will rather boast about my weaknesses, so that the power
> of Christ may dwell in me.... For when I am weak, then
> I am strong. (2 Corinthians 12:9–10)

Ronnie and Jill sat in my office unable to speak.
Ronnie eventually erupted with uncontrollable sobs, confess-

ing to an extramarital affair with a co-worker. Jill was devastated, not only because of her husband's betrayal, but because of her perceived failure as a wife. They were both certain that life as they knew it was over.

Since they were both Christians, I asked, "Have you ever considered the potential benefits of this experience?" They looked bewildered. Benefits? What possible good could come from a failure like this?

"God says that He strengthens us in our problems so that we can offer the same strength and encouragement to those who experience similar problems," I suggested. "If our whole reason for living on earth is to turn people to God, just think of all the people you will be able to help discover God's forgiveness! You can be Exhibit A of God's love and power to heal any relationship."

Ronnie and Jill left my office that afternoon convinced they had the possibility for a second act in their marriage. Although far different than what they would have chosen, they believed their second act could be as fulfilling as any they'd imagined.

You may be saying to yourself, "I'm not sure I like the role God has assigned to me. I want to be the star, not just some bit player on stage."

But before you reject the part God offers you, understand the payoff for playing your assigned role well.

THE REWARD: IT'S GREATER THAN YOU IMAGINE

Don't misunderstand. God doesn't reward failure. One day when you stand before Him, don't expect to hear, "You lost all your money in silver futures? Congratulations! I'll put you in charge of many kingdoms!" Nor can you expect to hear, "You cheated on your mate? Wonderful! Because you were unfaithful in your marriage, I'll grant you eternal riches."

However, God does reward you for connecting the whole of your life, including both successes and failures, to His eternal purpose of drawing people to Himself.

Just look at what He did for Jesus. Because Christ spent His entire life turning the spotlight away from Himself and focusing it on God the Father, God "highly exalted Him" (Philippians 2:9)—and He will do the same for you. "If we endure, we will also reign with Him" the Bible promises (2 Timothy 2:12).

No, there's no prize for failing. But when we ask God not only to forgive us but also to use our mistakes for His eternal purpose, the reward He offers is both unimaginable and unending.

In the final installment of the Chronicles of Narnia series, *The Last Battle,* C. S. Lewis illustrates the reality of God's indescribable and eternal rewards. Earlier in the story, the children are involved in a train wreck that dispatches them to the magical world of Narnia, which is a picture of heaven. When their adventure is drawing to a close, they express fear that they will be sent back to Earth. But the great lion, Aslan, a type of Jesus Christ, shares with them the wonderful news:

> "There was a real railway accident. Your father and mother and all of you are—as you used to call it in the Shadowlands—dead. The term is over: the holidays have begun. The dream is ended, this is the morning."

And as He spoke, He no longer looked to them like a
lion: but the things that began to happen after that were so
great and beautiful that I cannot write them. And for us
this is the end of all the stories, and we can most truly say
that they lived happily ever after. But for them it was only
the beginning of the real story. All their life in this world
and all their adventures in Narnia had only been the cover
and the title page: now at last they were beginning Chapter
One of the Great Story which no one on earth has read:
which goes on forever: in which every chapter is better than
the one before.[2]

Jesus said, "I give eternal life to them, and they will never per-
ish" (John 10:28). If you have trusted in Christ as your Savior,
your failure does not have to mark the end of your life. Even your
physical death doesn't bring the curtain down.

Everything you've experienced in your life so far—including
the failure that may still haunt you—is just a prelude to your second act.

And that second act can begin right now—and go on forever
and ever and ever.

Questions for Further Study

Chapter 1: When You Think It's Curtains!

1. What motivated you to purchase this book or begin this study? What do you hope to gain from this study? List all your reasons and expectations.

2. Cite one example of a slip-up and a mess-up in your life. What were the consequences, if any, of each?

3. Can you identify a major blowup in your life that seems to have unending consequences? If you're in a group, you don't need to share any details, but did your mistake involve a poor choice or a missed opportunity?

4. Do you agree or disagree with the author's statement that we're predisposed to make mistakes in life? Why or why not?

5. How would you respond to the statement "I don't think it's fair that God would condemn everyone for Adam's mistake"?

6. Reread the quote from Max Lucado on page 13. Why do we have a hard time believing that God really is crazy about us?

7. Do you agree with the author's premise that God not only forgives our mistakes but can use our mistakes for good? Why or why not?

8. The author cited several examples of people in the Bible whose failures became steppingstones for success. Think of one or two more examples from the Bible, and look up passages on those.

Chapter 2: Meet the Divine Director

1. Read Romans 8:31–39. What causes you to feel separated from God? What eternal truths do you find in the Romans passage that encourage you?

2. The author invites you to picture the biggest blowup in your life. Focus on that. What evidence is there that God is willing to forgive you for that mistake?

3. Read Matthew 6:14–15 and Ephesians 4:32. Is it possible to receive God's forgiveness and refuse to forgive other people? Why or why not?

4. Imagine a friend came to you with the following situation. "Last year I had an affair. After my husband discovered it, I immediately broke it off and asked for his and God's forgiveness. However, my husband still wants a divorce. If God has really forgiven me, why doesn't He restore my marriage?" How would you answer?

5. What's the difference between "covering" and "covering over" sin?

6. In Psalm 32:1–2, David uses three words to describe what God did for him: *forgiven, covered,* and *impute.* After reading the author's explanation of each word, which of these actions from God gives you the most relief? Why?

7. Does God's will for our lives include our mistakes, or does God simply take our mistakes and use them for good? What scriptures support your answer?

8. As you look back over your life, can you cite an example of God's transforming your failure?

Chapter 3: But Isn't the Script Already Written?

1. Reread the two stories that begin this chapter. How would you have answered the questions from Missy's daughter and from Bill?

2. How would you explain the term *God's sovereignty*? Do you really believe that God is in control over all His creation? Why or why not?

3. What is the relationship between God's will and our will? Does God ever influence or change a person's will? Explain and support your answer.

4. Do you believe that God has a detailed plan to encompass every aspect of your life, from whom you marry (or not) to what you eat for breakfast? Why or why not?

5. What would you say to someone who said, "I believe I missed God's will in the selection of a mate. I married the wrong person"?

6. How would you answer the question, "If God has a plan for my life that includes my mistakes, how can I be held responsible for those mistakes?"

7. Read Ephesians 1:11. What does this verse say about the belief that God has two wills: a perfect will and a permissive will?

139

8. After reading this chapter, how do you feel about the biggest mistake of your life?

Chapter 4: Fess Up to Your Mess-Up

1. Do you find it difficult to admit your mistakes? Why or why not?
2. Why is admission of failure a necessary first step to experiencing a second act?
3. Does admission of guilt always lead to forgiveness from others? Why or why not?
4. Reflect on a time in your life when you hit the emotional Reset button. What circumstances led you to make that decision? How do you keep from traveling back emotionally to your first-act mistake?
5. As you reflect on a major failure in your life, what's the most important lesson you learned from that mistake?
6. Do you agree with the author's statement that we can forgive only those people we're willing to blame? How do you keep blame from turning into bitterness?
7. Do you find it easy or difficult to forgive others? Why?
8. What new insights have you learned about receiving God's forgiveness and granting forgiveness to others?

Chapter 5: Don't Mess Up for Free

1. Why do you think people find it easier to repeat mistakes than to learn from their mistakes? Is there a mistake you find yourself consistently repeating? Why do you think you're prone to repeat that sin?

2. Do you think you tend to learn more from your successes or your failures? Why? Recount a valuable lesson you have learned from a major failure in your life.

3. Reread pages 78–80 about the three perspectives on failure: permanent or temporary, universal or specific, and internal or external. Which of these perspectives do you tend to embrace? Why do you think that is true? How can you change your perspective of failure?

4. Who in your circle of friends or acquaintances has experienced a major failure in the past year? What lesson can you learn from his or her mistake?

5. Would you find it easy or difficult to consult with someone after a major failure? Why? To whom would you turn for counsel after a personal failure? To whom would you turn for counsel about financial or vocational failure?

6. Identify another question, in addition to those the author lists, that you should ask someone else, yourself, or God after experiencing a failure.

7. How would you respond if your closest friend said, "I'm hesitant to bring this up, but I feel as if you're not giving the attention to your spouse that you should"? What can you do to ensure that those closest to you will tell you the truth about yourself and help you avoid a mistake?

8. Suppose one of your children said, "Tell me about the biggest mistake of your life and what you learned from it." Which failure would you feel comfortable sharing with your children and would benefit them the most?

Chapter 6: Enjoy Your Intermission

1. Why do you think intermissions differ in length for different people?

2. Have you ever experienced an intermission in life? If you had a choice (be honest with yourself), would you rather skip the intermission and go immediately from your first act to your second act? Why or why not?

3. Do you think you would profit more from an intermission in your twenties or in your fifties? Why?

4. Identify a mistake you or someone close to you made by trying to skip an intermission. How would an intermission have prevented that mistake?

5. How would you answer the questions on pages 101–2 that would help you reflect on the past and visualize your future?

6. Are you comfortable with solitude? When in the next thirty days could you schedule several hours alone to follow the author's suggestions on page 104 for renewing your relationship with God? Where would you go? What arrangements do you need to make in order to schedule that time alone with God?

7. Who in your circle of relationships is experiencing an intermission in life? Without preaching a sermon to him or her, what encouragement could you offer about an intermission you have experienced?

8. Why do you think God rarely tells us ahead of time how long our intermissions will last?

Chapter 7: Begin Your Second Act Now

1. What regret do you find yourself repeatedly reliving? Why does this regret haunt you more than others?

2. How do you understand the biblical passage that says God remembers our iniquities no more (see Jeremiah 31:34 and Hebrews 8:12)? Can God actually forget our failures? If not, what does this verse mean?

3. Think about a major change you have experienced. What signs, if any, preceded that change? Why does God sometimes signal an approaching change and other times not?

4. Do you sense an approaching transition in your life? If so, why? What can you do to prepare for it?

5. What's the difference between planning for our futures and presuming upon the future? Do you tend to plan for the future? Why or why not?

6. Return to pages 115–16 and develop a script that will help you deal with a mistake you have made. Make sure your script includes clarification of the problem, visualization of the goal, identification of the obstacles, and specification of action steps.

7. Identify one area in your life in which you need to move forward, despite limited visibility. What makes you hesitant about traveling in a fog, so to speak?

8. Take a moment to reflect on the question "In twenty years what will you wish you had done today?" What is the first thought that comes to mind? What is the first step you should take today?

Chapter 8: Prepare for the Grand Finale

1. Reread 1 Corinthians 4:9. Before reading this book, did you view your life as a performance or spectacle to the visible and invisible world? What impressions or insights does that image give you?

2. Imagine that God freeze-framed your life story and then turned to the angels and asked, "What do you think about him or her so far?" How do you think the angels would respond?

3. Take a moment to draw a time line of your life up to this point, indicating three or four milestone events (successes or failures). How does the fact that you are going to live forever color your perspective about those events?

4. Since you are going to live forever, does it make any difference whether your failure occurs early or later in life? Why or why not?

5. Reread the statement "It does not matter how well you do what you do, if you do not do what you should do." Do you have a clear understanding of the assignment God has given you? How does the knowledge of your assignment affect your attitude toward these various roles you play?

    Husband or wife: _____

    Employee or employer: _____

    Citizen: _____

    Parent: _____

    Church member: _____

6. Recount an instance in which a failure in your life or in the life of someone you know resulted in God's glorification.
7. Read 2 Corinthians 5:10 and 1 Corinthians 3:10–15. If your earthly life were to end right now, how do you think God would judge your life? What can you start doing differently today to ensure your rewards in heaven?
8. What's the most valuable insight you have gained from this book?

Notes

Chapter 1: When You Think It's Curtains!

1. Cited in David Jeremiah, *Slaying the Giants in Your Life* (Nashville: W Publishing, 2001), 173.
2. Les Brown (Spiritually Motivated Seminar, Hyatt Regency, Dallas, TX, November 11, 2002).
3. Max Lucado, *A Gentle Thunder: Hearing God Through the Storm* (Nashville: W Publishing, a division of Thomas Nelson Inc., 1995), 121–22. Reprinted by permission. All rights reserved.

Chapter 2: Meet the Divine Director

1. Carlo Walth, "The God of Second Chances," *Youthworker* (March–April 1999), www.Youthspecialties.com.
2. Max Lucado, *Cure for the Common Life: Living in Your Sweet Spot* (Nashville: W Publishing, a division of Thomas Nelson Inc., 2005), 69–70. Reprinted by permission. All rights reserved.
3. Gordon MacDonald, "Transforming Failure," *Discipleship Journal*, no. 109 (January–February 1999): 58.
4. Charles W. Colson, *Loving God* (Grand Rapids: Zondervan, 1983), 24.

Chapter 3: But Isn't the Script Already Written?

1. W. A. Criswell, *Ephesians: An Exposition* (Grand Rapids: Zondervan, 1974), 28–29.

2. Charles R. Swindoll, *David: A Man of Passion & Destiny: Profiles in Character* (Dallas: Word Publishing, 1997), 15.

3. Harold Myra and Marshall Shelley, *The Leadership Secrets of Billy Graham* (Grand Rapids: Zondervan, 2005), 186–87, and www.jcpenney.net.

4. Myra and Shelley, *The Leadership Secrets of Billy Graham*, 199.

Chapter 4: Fess Up to Your Mess-Up

1. Gordon MacDonald, "Transforming Failure," *Discipleship Journal,* no. 109 (January–February 1999), 58.

2. William Manchester, *The Last Lion: Winston Spencer Churchill* (Boston: Little, Brown, 1983), 25.

3. Timothy Jones, *Finding a Spiritual Friend: How Friends and Mentors Can Make Your Faith Grow* (Nashville: Upper Room Books, 1998), 34.

4. Carlo Walth, "The God of Second Chances," *Youthworker* (March–April 1999), www.Youthspecialties.com.

5. John C. Maxwell, *Failing Forward: Turning Mistakes into Stepping-Stones for Success* (Nashville: Thomas Nelson, 2000), 53.

6. John Ortberg, *If You Want to Walk on Water, You've Got to Get Out of the Boat* (Grand Rapids: Zondervan, 2001), 22.

7. Ortberg, *If You Want to Walk on Water,* 22.

8. Lewis B. Smedes, *The Art of Forgiving: When You Need to Forgive and Don't Know How* (New York: Ballantine, 1996), 178.

Chapter 5: Don't Mess Up for Free

1. Peter Biskind, "Reconstructing Woody," *Vanity Fair,* December 2005, 326. Reprinted by permission of International Creative Management Inc. Copyright © 2005 by Peter Biskind.

2. Nelson Boswell, quoted in John C. Maxwell, *The Success Journey* (Nashville: Thomas Nelson, 1997), 127–28.

3. Martin E. P. Seligman, *Learned Optimism* (New York, Alfred A. Knopf, 1990), 44.

4. Seligman, *Learned Optimism,* 46.

5. Biskind, "Reconstructing Woody," 327.

6. Seligman, *Learned Optimism,* 49.

7. Sydney Finkelstein, interview by Jennifer Merritt, "The ABCs of Failure," *Business Week,* June 9, 2003, 126.

8. Derek Kidner, *Proverbs: An Introduction and Commentary* (Downers Grove, IL: InterVarsity Press, 1964), 43.

9. Charles Swindoll, comp., *The Tale of the Tardy Oxcart and 1,501 Other Stories* (Nashville: Word Publishing, 1998), 321–22.

10. Giles Kemp and Edward Claflin, *Dale Carnegie: The Man Who Influenced Millions* (New York: St. Martin's, 1989), 134–35.

Chapter 6: Enjoy Your Intermission

1. Blaise Pascal, *Pensées: The Provincial Letters* (New York: Random House, 1941), 48–49.

2. John Ortberg, *If You Want to Walk on Water, You've Got to Get Out of the Boat* (Grand Rapids: Zondervan, 2001), 151.

Chapter 7: Begin Your Second Act Now

1. Erwin Raphael McManus, *Seizing Your Divine Moment: Dare to Live a Life of Adventure* (Nashville: Thomas Nelson, 2002), 16.

2. Harold S. Kushner, *When All You've Ever Wanted Isn't Enough* (New York: Simon & Schuster, 1965), 58–59.

3. Leonard W. Labaree and others, eds., *The Autobiography of Benjamin Franklin* (New Haven: Yale University Press, 1964), 163.

4. McManus, *Seizing Your Divine Moment,* 16.

5. Charles Spurgeon, quoted in David Jeremiah, *Slaying the Giants in Your Life* (Nashville: W Publishing, 2001), 153–54.

Chapter 8: Prepare for the Grand Finale

1. Kenneth Ulmer, main session presentation at Leadership Summit 2005, Willow Creek Association, Barrington, Illinois, August 12, 2005 (compact disc).

2. C. S. Lewis, *The Last Battle,* in *The Chronicles of Narnia* (New York: Harper Collins, 2001), 767.

About the Author

ROBERT JEFFRESS is a best-selling author of sixteen books, including *The Divine Defense, The Solomon Secrets, Grace Gone Wild!* and *Hell? Yes!* He has served as senior pastor of the ten-thousand-member First Baptist Church of Wichita Falls, Texas, since 1992. He is a graduate of Baylor University and Dallas Theological Seminary and earned his doctorate at Southwestern Baptist Theological Seminary. Dr. Jeffress hosts the weekly radio and television program *Pathway to Victory,* aired on more than a thousand television stations and cable systems and in numerous countries around the world.

ALSO BY ROBERT JEFFRESS

The Divine Defense

Coming Home

Hell? Yes! And Other Outrageous Truths You Can Still Believe

Grace Gone Wild!

The Solomon Secrets

Hearing the Master's Voice

When Forgiveness Doesn't Make Sense

I Want More!

About the Author's Ministries

FIRST BAPTIST CHURCH of Wichita Falls, Texas, is an evangelical Christian church whose mission is to spread the good news of Jesus Christ and lead people to become obedient and reproducing disciples of Jesus Christ, as He commanded in Matthew 28:18–20.

The church conducts many ministries, from small-group Bible studies (LIFE Groups—Learning, Involving, Fellowshiping, and Evangelizing) and prayer and recovery groups, to community outreach, to women's and teen ministries. Learn more about the church online at the First Baptist Church Web site: http://www.fbcwf.org.

To tune into the teaching ministry of Dr. Robert Jeffress, check out *Pathway to Victory,* a nationally broadcast program currently seen on Faith TV on Saturday nights at 6 p.m. (CST), on Family Net TV on Sundays at noon (CST), and on the Daystar Network on Sunday afternoons at 1:30 p.m. (CST). To order tapes from the *Pathway* archive, call toll-free 1-800-348-TAPE. You may listen to the daily radio broadcast at www.ptv.org.

Designed to provide insight on the truth found in God's Word, *Pathway to Victory* aims to give viewers and listeners practical application of God's Word for everyday life through clear, biblical teaching. To download free messages or subscribe to the free monthly newsletter, *Path Lights,* log on to www.ptv.org.